MIDLIFE AWAKENING

Start with this.

By Michael Blizman

MICHAEL BLIZMAN

Copyright © 2020 Michael Blizman.

Written by Michael Blizman.

Published by HouSolutions LLC

While every precaution has been taken in the preparation of this book, the publisher assumes no responsibility for errors or omissions, or for damages resulting from the use of the information contained herein.

MIDLIFE AWAKENING

First edition. October 10, 2019.

TABLE OF CONTENTS

Acknowledgements
PREFACE
Introduction
Avoidance and Friends
   How Did I Get Here? (Slowly)
   It's All You, Baby
   Dissatisfied? It's still all you...
What to Fix First?
The Easy Stuff
The Hard Stuff
We are Not Separated...Now What?
Mindset, a Small key to a Big Door
Your Mindset is not a Secret
Chinks in the Armor (I don't need armor)
People around us are mirrors
Enter, The Shadow
Approaching the Goal Line, but Still not Feeling Like a Winner
Changes are Coming
It is OK to Want What You Want
Tuning in to a quiet voice

DISCOVERY
Epiphany 1: It is right for me to be happy
Epiphany 2: It is right to begin as soon as you feel the desire
Epiphany 3: I am Completely Responsible for My Life
Epiphany 4: Feeling better is the main thing I can do
Epiphany 5: My thoughts determine how I experience life

THE PAGE TURNS AND EMOTIONS SUCK
Are you Stuck?

YOU KNOW WHAT YOUR PROBLEM IS?
It's Serious, but not *that* Serious
Look for patterns first
Integration versus Divide and Conquer
Acknowledge Small Victories
How long can you take to solve your big problem?
What is holding you back?
One Source of Troubles - I should...

Another Source of Trouble - Our Thoughts
What is a Thought?
What is Your Mind Trying to Do?
Thoughts You Have Often, Form Beliefs
Thoughts are Addictive
Thoughts are Hyperlinked
How to Break the Negative Thought Cycle
Beliefs
It's Easier to Look at Someone's Splinter
Questions
Habits
Expectations
Your Standards
Focus: Whatever we focus on, we get more of
Acknowledging our emotions and accepting ourselves
What Works
   Practice: Journaling
   Practice: Meditating
   Practice: Re-program
   Practice: Rest
   Practice: Eat well
   Practice: Move
   Practice: Surrounding yourself with good people
   Practice: Read
   Practice: Smile
   Outcomes of "the practices"
Connecting the Dots
   Things I have learned along the way:
Closing Thoughts

ACKNOWLEDGEMENTS

I am grateful for the experience and the patience of my family and friends as we all make our journey through this life. We are all teachers to one another.

Special thanks to David Siudmak for creating the book cover art. Special thanks also to Nolan and Peggy Rome for their interest in improving this book with detailed edit suggestions and helpful feedback and discussion.

This book would not have been possible, had it not been for the work of all those who came before me. As I approached spinouts in my life, my direction was corrected along the way, influenced by all the greats, whose material has guided so many including me.

My hope is that my specific experience with these ideas and practices will add value to at least one person who otherwise may have missed their on-ramp to awakening. My gratitude to such authors, speakers, idea-gatherers, and philosophers as Rumi, Wayne Dwyer, Bruce L, Marcus Aurelius, Tony Robbins, Brendon Burchard, Tim Ferris, Les Brown, Napoleon Hill, Earl Nightingale, Jen Sincero, Abraham Hicks, Laozi, Paulo Coelho, Viktor Frankl, Eckhart Tolle, Peter Diamondis, and Robert Greene.

PREFACE

This book took over 2 years to write, which started after about two and a half years of working on myself intensely. Over the two and a half years of trying to fix my thinking and my life, I read over forty books related to philosophy, religion, metaphysics, and self-help. I also tried numerous techniques, activities and practices including meditation, super-disciplined gym workouts, traditional prayer, subliminal recordings, motivational speakers, and every other thing that helped anyone I encountered.

Through journaling along the way, I was able to track the ideas and practices which I found most helpful. I also noticed that some ideas were common across multiple philosophies, books, and even religions. This information from my journals became the basis of this book.

I chose the subtitle of this book, "Start with this", because I believe that this book can serve as a useful introduction of concepts and helpful ideas to try for people who are beginning a transformative experience, and the narratives in the book tend to document my raw state of being as I began my search.

I ran into some challenges while writing this book, especially as I began to share parts of it with friends to get their opinions. As a software developer, I mostly read technical material, so I tend to think and write in a procedural style with no extra descriptions or background. I just want to get an outcome in the best way possible. A friend of mine mentioned that although I am a software architect by trade, and prefer brevity, most humans find some personal anecdotes and narrative helpful to absorb useful information, so I shared some details to show how an idea affected me as a person, not just what I did to get to an outcome.

I had a teacher in 8th grade who encouraged us to raise our hands and ask questions. She said, "...this is a big class, and if you do not understand something and have a question, there is a good chance someone else has the same question, so please ask your question because it will help you and help others." Well, the world is a big place, and if I learned something the long and difficult way, maybe someone else can learn their important lessons a bit easier or faster by reading this, if I raise my hand and share my own questions and experiences. My hope is that this book will:

1. Help you recognize issues you are experiencing as soon as possible

2. Provide reassurance that you are not the only one who has gone through something similar

3. Share some ideas about how to start improving things immediately

Hints for different styles of readers

Many of us like to read fast and skip over things that are not immediately of interest. I tried to support both of those reading styles. So, you can read this book front to back and absorb the narratives and take-aways as they arrive in the chapters. If you are a reader who prefers to skim first, then dive into points of interest, look for emphasized text that is between paragraphs and centered, something like this:

This is a really important point, so maybe go back a paragraph or two to get the context to see if it resonates for you

Then continue on with your reading please. I hope you enjoy it.

INTRODUCTION

My preference is to avoid digging up the past. None of it can be changed, and it is common when we review the events of the past, to trigger old feelings and thoughts which are not helpful at all. Some examples of this include justifying why you did what you did or how you got to be where you are now. None of that matters. The only thing that matters is what you want *now* and what you are going to do *now*.

To put an even sharper point on this, what you experienced in the past and the person you were when you made those decisions does not exist anymore except in your memory and imagination. Even the person you were 6 months ago is an imaginary thing today, unless you have stopped growing or changing during that time. It is impossible to stay neutral; you are either growing or shrinking. The only thing that matters is what you are going to do now. There is no way to act in the future or to act in the past, only now.

Looking back is only useful to determine how you might have handled something better, or to recognize that situation as something you must accept. Still, a little review or history of the experiences that led me to writing this book might be of interest or resonate with you. On the other hand, you may simply want to dive into the practical application of the ideas and practices which I found so very helpful. Feel free to skip to the next chapter or to any chapter that interests you. For those who need the back story, here we go, as briefly as I can muster, my obligatory introduction.

I was profoundly unhappy for years with seriously vacant, sagging relationships, and a massive drop in my overall motivation level. We can summarize it by saying that I had some symptoms of depression. I was still doing well professionally, but work was the only area of my life that was not obviously suffering. I had been toying around with ways to improve the way I felt about my life for some time. Around the end of 2015 I started recognizing an inner pull to change the way I was, and how I was living. I was emotionally flat, generally not enjoying life, and all my relationships were stagnating. I sensed that I was going to hit an even lower low soon. If I went any lower, it would be new territory for me, and I thought that hitting that low would likely start to affect my job performance and income, on top of me just feeling lousy like I had become accustomed. My mind was buzzing with chaotic and many negative thoughts and expectations. Say what you will about traditional roles...I know that if I hit a low that could jeopardize my ability to provide for my family, I would feel really, really bad...maybe to the point where I just would decide not to play this game anymore. This realization pulled me into a promise to myself that I would do whatever is needed to make changes in my life, so I could avoid that low, and start to become the person I want to be. I would change regardless of who or what I would need to let go, what pain I was going to feel, or who else was going to be affected. While this next thought is dramatic, I was fine with dying in the attempt of this, because the thing that mattered most was to get out of whatever mode I was in. I had to be willing to look at everything and everyone in my life and decide how much of each of those people and things I would allow to occupy my life. I knew that if I did not do this, I would not be able to cut through the noise of my mind and figure out what I really want or need to do next. I had to find a way back to myself, and there was no longer space in my life for any sacred cows. I knew deep down that if I did not start now, soon there would be nothing left of me, and I would likely fail at even the most basic of my roles as a parent and provider for my children.

AVOIDANCE AND FRIENDS

Talking with trusted friends or advisors or therapists can help give us clarity, new ideas, and perspective. A lot of people, especially men, and definitely me, had not built those close relationships with friends or mentors. A part of me wishes that I had built those relationships before I ran into trouble because it may have really helped me redirect and refocus sooner and avoid some problems that continued to grow over an extended time. Instead, I stuffed everything I was feeling down just to avoid uncertainty and discomfort.

Based on what I have learned over the past couple years, I would recommend that men invest some time in building friendships. It doesn't have to be like an episode of Oprah or Dr. Phil. As a ridiculous, testosterone-buffered example, what if you have a 20 second exchange about a problem you are having with your buddy, but at the end of an hour spent at the shooting range? If you find out that he had something similar happen to him and tried he tried this or that, it could mean a big difference to the quality of your life. You might find out that your buddy is struggling in his marriage or you might even get a good idea or two about how to talk to your significant other in a way that could help you, or you could feel at least like you are normal and connected and not some socially backward freak.

One time I was with my business partner and friend, and I mentioned that my wife had a bad dream about me which she shared. In the dream she described something she did which was a bit silly or strange, and how I got totally angry and frustrated with her in that dream. Dave suggested that if his wife shared something like that with him, he would have replied to his wife, "Sorry hon, I really could have handled that better [in your dream]." Embracing the absurdity is completely hilarious and disarming. I wish I would have had that one ready when the moment was upon, but maybe next time because I picked up a new way from my friend. The point is that by talking to other people, you might discover some approaches that will help you later on. Learning from others will save you time and trouble.

How Did I Get Here? (Slowly)

Everybody grows at their own pace. Building habits that result in having friends or mentors does not happen automatically. It is going to take some time to get comfortable talking to others about what is going on in your life. In about 2009, my wife and I were having marital problems. In hindsight, it could have been helpful for to me to confront what I was feeling and experiencing in those days, and to have someone to talk about it with in a way that did not seem strange. It might have been helpful to get another perspective on things, no matter how awkward that would have been with the limited self-awareness and communication skills I possessed at that time.

At the time, I did not think it was necessary to confront some difficult topics head on, and it was more convenient to put them off and continue doing what I normally did every day. As a result, our relationship stopped growing. I also did not build friendships with other men. I really did not even realize that I was missing out, until I started paying attention to acquaintances and new friends, and how they were getting along.

Since those times, I have become more deliberately open with people that I consider friends and it has been a great change in my life. This starts with some vulnerability that can feel uncomfortable at first. It was not easy for me, as I tend to have this natural tendency or old belief that I was supposed to have everything all worked out and do new things perfectly the first time I try them. It takes some experience and attention to build the confidence to know that you do not have to have everything figured out in order to start. It's OK to bumble at something new and to improve over time. Trying to reach out to people is not easy or risk free either. Several times I tested the waters with people I associated with to see if they were open to becoming better friends. These were men about my age who had kids the same age and in similar activities. Most of these men were not open at all. I think that a whole lot of men are not receptive to deeper friendships because many of us have accepted a lie that we are weak if we cannot solve all our problems on our own or if our lives are not perfect.

Comparing and learning from other men could help you develop your relationship skills faster. These men, like me did not have any of the tools, any of the experience, or any of the knowledge to see how things are going or how much better things could go if we all would just open up a bit. They were doing exactly what they knew how to do, and being what they knew how to be, nothing more, nothing less. Sometimes, because of my level of maturity perhaps, I thought "what is wrong with that guy" because he acted like a jerk. Perhaps I felt like I should be more put together, but as time went by, I discovered some of those dudes I reached out to were totally closed off and heading into their own storm of life. They are just like me, with only variances in their specific experiences. When I look around now, I see a whole bunch of men who are a bit lost, heading toward a bad situation, and completely lacking anyone in their life who could offer some useful perspective. Many of us have no vocabulary to even ask for help. We don't even recognize the usefulness of that other perspective. If you can be open with some other men, you can get ahead faster. It's because you get to learn from each other and not go through every problem yourself to get the wisdom that comes from experience.

If you are planning to live 600 years, you might have time to make all your own mistakes and learn from them, but for the rest of us, we might want to learn from other people and save ourselves some time and some pain

Something I found out from speaking to other men since this time, is that many of us follow a similar pattern. I had neglected friendships and other areas of my life that would have provided emotional support for me during a suffering marriage or approaching divorce. Even before the threat of divorce, I now believe that if I had relationships with other experienced men, I might have noticed my marriage issues sooner and received some useful suggestions from those men before it hit the crisis point. With a lack of experience, it is hard to be sure if a problem is a really big one, or just one of those minor disagreements that happen when two people are together a lot and going through life together. With perspective from others, I might have believed that I could improve things instead of feeling powerless. Instead of building my life and friendships while married, I did a lot of things that I believed were my duty, and I ignored friendships. I ignored play, and all those things which did not directly serve work or family. But these are the things that contribute to a rich life and make you a better person to be around. For a long while, I actually felt guilty if I took a half hour to myself to do something I enjoy or spent money on things that were for me.

Some people like lists, so for emphasis, and not for self-loathing, I list below some of the critical mistakes I made:

1. I did not build friendships with other men.

Being married can be a complicated thing. If you can compare experiences with someone else, you might be able to level-up your skills and be a better husband and father. Books and online mentors count and can help too.

2. I let things get bad enough for long enough that I felt powerless to change things.

My confidence dropped low. If you feel powerless, you stop trying.

3. I ignored play.

Doing stuff just for the fun, joy and laughter is how you relieve stress, create good stories to share, and have a life you enjoy. Make time for this.

4. Felt guilt for doing anything that was just for my own enjoyment.

This is dumb. Read a book you want to read. Go play pickup basketball with your own friends. Let your family know it's OK to do that. They will learn it's OK and pursue their own interests too. If you can include your family during some of your activities, that is good too.

There was always something that needed to be done, or someone that wanted something. This is not something that others put on me, but something I thought was part of my job as a parent or husband for whatever reason. The result is that over time, I became unhappy and had very little meaningful social interactions with anyone except my spouse. Relying upon her to run the social aspects of life, coordinate activities with the kids, and anticipate other needs is way too much to expect from anyone. First, we are all responsible for finding our own path to happiness, and second, another person cannot possibly get all that right.

Nobody can do a good job of making another person happy.

When I started to notice I was not feeling right, even though I was not fully aware of the feelings of anger or resentment until later, I found myself stuffing down those feelings. Maybe my discontent was caused by me not living a life I enjoyed. I did not think it was important enough to pursue my interests, because I listened to that critical voice in my head that repeated things like, "...the job pays for all this," and "...the kids come first." You can insert your own excuse for not living your own life here, but it is all caused by the same thing—You did not think it important to pursue your own interests and values. Perhaps if I had a more experienced friend, he would have pointed out sooner that what I was feeling was not going to correct itself, and it was not something that I should accept as normal.

IT'S ALL YOU, BABY

While the perspective of others can be helpful, you own your life. You are the only one who can fix it. The truth is, you have all the knowledge, experience and skill necessary to move your life in a better direction. You don't have to get everything perfect on the first try either...you can take it one step at a time.

I encourage everyone to build some friendships, but let's shift back and deal with how things are going for you right now. Rest assured that you can start being open to new friends now and have a better future. For now, let's get moving with how things are right now.

For those of you who are in a situation like I was in, you are where you are, and you have to deal with life, even if you have no close friends or mentors to turn to at the moment. This situation is a lot like you might have experienced at your work...you are in crunch time and the project is in full swing, and there is no time to hire the people you probably should have hired 3 months ago to meet your timelines. You are likely in a storm and do not have anyone nearby with answers to help you figure it all out.

Here is the thing though: You probably already know what needs to be done, you just don't want to do it because it's more work or discomfort than you want to take on. Outside of work, we feel the same things sometimes. You have a situation in your life that is not pleasant to work through, and you are doubting yourself. You probably either know what to do or know enough to take one step in the right direction, if you can tune into your own feelings about it. One thing I find helpful is to get your feelings in front of your eyes so you can know what is going on. You do not have to share any of your feelings yet, but you do have to know what they are or at least partly know. You can get to know your own feelings spending time in lots of ways. If you need to go for a 10 mile walk to get some quiet time, do it. If you need to go for long drive, that is fine too. If you can write out what is going on and what you are noticing, that can give you clarity too. You don't have to solve every part of the problem, but first step is to figure out what you are experiencing if you are not quite clear about it yet. Take your own counsel first. Once you have spent some time with yourself, you might have a wave of thoughts and feeling rising in you. Writing some of those down will help you clarify them. If you are new to this, try this out: When writing, pretend you are explaining what you feel right now to a best friend who already knows your background so you don't have to explain your whole life or justify anything…you just have to briefly jot down what you are experiencing right now. This will help you see the situation outside of your own head, on paper. Not any better than it is, and not any worse.

Have you ever talked to someone who seemed to want advice, and you listen to them dutifully, then carefully express what you think they should do or share your perspective, only to have them completely ignore your perfect advice and do something else anyway? Your friend ignoring your advice may be frustrating but consider this perspective: Maybe you were giving advice to yourself.

A lot of times, talking to other people only has value because it forces you to slow down and organize your thoughts enough to convey to someone else.

By the time you get the words out, you are often already sensing how to solve your own issue or the next step at least. The opinion of the person you are talking to might not even matter.

MICHAEL BLIZMAN

I will go further to say that if you build a habit of taking some quiet time, even going for long walks by yourself with no distractions, you can talk to yourself as you walk, and gain a lot of clarity on your situation, as long as you are not criticizing yourself too. While another person's perspective can be helpful, I want to emphasize this next point for all of you who feel that you do not have anyone who you are comfortable with to talk to about your problems:

> *You yourself are the most qualified person to notice when you have a problem, to identify that problem, and to find a way to get past that problem.*

Deep down, you know how you feel about everything, even if you have been denying it, or avoiding it for a very long time. Even if you do not think you *should* feel some way about it. Sometimes we lose trust in our own preferences or stuff all of those down to deal with later, until we *almost* forget what is there. You need to keep your own counsel. If you have someone you trust to get an opinion, go ahead and talk about it, but your own idea about how to handle is likely the best one and the one you should weigh the most. Writing things down really helps you to clarify what you are experiencing.

Once you have clarity about your situation, you can breathe for a bit and think about something else for a bit. Take a nap, take shower, go for a bike ride, whatever. Give a little time for ideas or possible solutions to bubble up on their own.

One other suggestion is not to feel like you have to rush into confrontations. If you are not sure what the next step to take is, do not feel like you have to do anything right now. You can wait, pray, trust that the right direction will be revealed to you, and you can stay open to it. Have a little faith, as you have already been guided to identifying what you are feeling and experiencing, which is a positive thing. I have found that situations seem to be designed to get our attention when necessary.

If you are too uncomfortable to face some problem or inconsistency in the way you are living or don't know what to do, there is no need to worry.

The problem you are ignoring may continue to grow until it gets big enough that you finally decide you have to deal with it, and until some specific action you take feels better than waiting.

You can either deal with it early or wait until you hit bottom or anywhere in between. You will know when you have enough clarity to act. The time you decide to deal with what is bugging you is your choice, and you do not have to push anything.

Dissatisfied? It's still all you...

If you are not satisfied or happy most of the time, what are you doing over there? Do you even know what would make you feel more satisfaction? If you are not satisfied, it's because:

You are living according to values that you accepted from someone else instead of what you really want.

If you are going to make an error, error on the side of taking too much responsibility for the conditions in your life. Try on the belief that everything is your fault or credit.

Perhaps you had a life event shake your confidence and shift you to a focus on fear. Not living your best life can be from a number of causes including feeling like you are less than others, fear triggered by some significant event, or beliefs you accepted from others (blame your parents here!). No matter why you are like this, the truth is exactly the same:

If you are not enjoying your life, it's because you do not feel like it is OK to create a life based on your values and your preferences.

WHAT TO FIX FIRST?

You might notice something really big going wrong in your life. You also might not think you can fix that right now for whatever reason. You also probably have a bunch of other things that could use some attention or correction. With your current level of angst, you might just as well pick something and make some progress.

In my case, I had marriage problems and financial problems. I decided to fix some money issues because they are not too complicated. Relationships are much more complicated, and I did not see a clear path to resolving those. Solving the easy stuff first leaves a big mountain at the end of your path. The main advantage to solving simpler problems first is that when you get to the base of the remaining mountain, your backpack will be lighter since those little problems will be handled. Another advantage of solving the simple first is that you can gain some confidence in your abilities to solve problems by handling them first.

The disadvantage to handling the simpler stuff first is that the only way to get past the harder subjects is to go through them and figure out what you really want. As long as you are focused on one thing, you are not focusing on the other, so you basically are kicking the big issue down the road.

THE EASY STUFF

On top of the underground resentment and unhappiness that I was feeling, we had created some very serious financial issues. To fix these financial issues, I had begun doing programming/consulting work on the side to pay off the debts and was working a lot of hours. Sure, some of these clients were not a great fit for me long-term. Some I discovered from Craigslist ads. One of those from Craigslist was quite a good client that I worked with for several years. Others, I would only work with on one, small project. Spreading mostly via word-of-mouth, I tackled a lot of projects for a good number of clients. Before I started doing the side consulting work, I also looked into basic part time jobs at home improvement stores and some other things. The consulting work was easier to work into my schedule, and paid much better, but due to similarity to my day job, increased my likelihood of burning out.

THE HARD STUFF

Working through relationship issues is much harder than solving money problems. Both people have to participate in a relationship. Both must have a compatible vision or approach for how to fix things, and both should try to not re-activate all the issues that lead to the problems in the first place. If one or the other is exhausted, or not open, or unwilling to try different ways to meet in the middle, the whole thing is frustrating and will feel like a waste of energy.

We had developed some relationship issues along the way, which lead to my wife desiring a divorce in 2009. At that time, we did some therapy but had different desired outcomes for therapy, which made the experience pretty bad. I refer back to the idea that both people need to have a similar vision for how to fix things. In this case, I did not want a divorce and she did, which as you might imagine, made therapy quite unpleasant for me especially, most of the time.

Anytime you want something and do not believe you can have it; you are going to feel bad.

Some good came out of the therapy anyway, probably because when you have nothing to lose, you are free to express yourself more. It's kind of like how being completely at the end of your rope and a bit crazy really frees you up by letting you ignore expectations and social norms. One benefit was that eventually I did express some emotions in a very visceral way when I accepted that she was not changing her mind about the divorce. I stopped resisting what was happening, and I accepted it. I let go of my marriage emotionally and accepted we would not be together, and I would have to figure out how to help my kids through this. My focus changed from what I was going through to what I could do to serve my kids most. Over the next few months, my wife and I would meet for lunch to discuss how the divorce would look, terms, etc. The nature of these discussions led to some productive communication and problem solving. Over this time, my wife stopped most of the behaviors that had really been aggravating me. We got a bit better at talking and planning the divorce in a reasonable way. As strange as all this seems, at a certain point, we were getting along fairly well, and we decided to not get divorced.

WE ARE NOT SEPARATED...NOW WHAT?

With a lack of experience in these matters, we really did not discuss terms of staying together, expectations, etc. We just tried to get along and not get divorced but did not get clarity about what each of us wanted.

I think the combination of fear of what a divorce would do to my kids emotionally and to our financial situation, getting back to a comfort zone, and the emotional exhaustion from the whole ordeal led to even more complacency in both of us. I learned in a very direct way that making life decisions based on what you want to avoid rather than what you want might be less than optimal (go ahead and say "duh" if you have to, I am kind of a slow learner in some areas). Since I saw no way to change my marriage at this point, and because our financial situation was pretty scary, I decided to first focus on resolving the big debt problem we had by working extra jobs as a consultant. I knew I could fix that problem by earning more money and controlling spending. Making money, is done by finding something you can sell, and then selling it, even if you are only selling your time at a job...It is simple! Fixing a relationship is a lot harder, as it requires some common vocabulary and rules for arguing, among other cooperative behaviors between the couple. Perhaps most importantly, it requires a belief that you can have a good relationship. Holding an empowering belief about a relationship that is going badly for a long time is pretty hard, probably because there you have so much intense and recent experience and evidence that it will not work out all around you that you see every day.

At that time, I did not believe I could have an honest, significant discussion or resolution with my wife about serious issues, without it devolving into a fight or crying or some other version of having no peace again. Over the years a pattern emerged in which when I held an opinion or perspective that differed from hers, I felt uncomfortable and judged. This is not to say she was to blame for this, but it was my experience and feeling at that time. Another way to say it is that I believed I was essentially powerless to fix my marriage or fully enjoy my home life.

If you believe you are powerless, you will stop trying.

This belief led to a lot of changes in the way I approached most areas of my life for a number of years. I worked a lot. Work was the only thing that was predictable. When I put energy and time in, I got money out to fix the debt problem. I became a very isolated person emotionally, even though I was high functioning in my professional life. In most ways, even when things were rough in my personal life, I kicked ass in my professional life. As I mentioned earlier, I did not have anyone that I wanted to talk with about what I was experiencing. So, for a very long time, I only had the voices in my own head to talk to over important personal things.

When you are in a bit of a downward spiral, that voice in your head is not usually a good person to rely on for great advice.

I tuned out the critical voice, which was growing louder each week by working, drinking one or two in the evening while working, and pushing myself into a lot of activities to stay busy all the time. I was completely unbalanced in my life, and I was getting even further out of touch with how I was feeling. It became very difficult to connect to other people in a real way, but a certain longing for a connection was still underneath, and unfulfilled. That is a long-winded way to say, I was lonely. In order to continue my plan to pay down the debt, I stuffed down those feelings of loneliness, powerlessness, and deep sadness. After four years of working 60 to 90-hour weeks in combination of a full-time corporate job, and a mostly one-man consulting practice, the main debt emergency was resolved, but I was spent. I let most of my client work go and took about 2 years off from big side projects unless the project really helped someone or was really interesting for some reason. This gets us caught up to about 2013.

MINDSET, A SMALL KEY TO A BIG DOOR

I learned this one the hard way. With the right focus and mindset, almost anything is possible, and with the wrong focus and mindset, everything is harder than it has to be.

A few years ago, I had been approaching the problem of paying down debt from a perspective of what was lacking and "I need to fix this". I was focused on removing the anchor, rather than sailing to paradise. I did not want my family to lower our lifestyle because I let our finances get out of control. I felt like requiring changes in our lifestyle would make me look like less in the eyes of my family.

Today, I like to believe that every problem has a solution or is an opportunity to grow. If approached the right way, I think I could have talked with my family constructively to reduce expenses. We probably could have arrived at some agreement and understanding to cut expenses in a way that my family would have felt like they were part of the process and the goal of becoming financially stable. I did not have to try to carry it all on my shoulders. I did not have to beat myself up so much for so long.

YOUR MINDSET IS NOT A SECRET

The people around you notice what you are feeling and thinking...It is not a secret. I am not saying that they can read your mind, but they can read your mood and how you are projecting yourself into every situation. There is some science around this, which revolves around the electromagnetic signals associated with thought and emotion which are detectable at a distance. Instinctively, you might sense this as a vibe you get from a person or in a room of people.

Problems don't stay all on one person's shoulders, because the people you live with notice you are changing and trying to do something and can feel anxiety because they do not know how to help. In hindsight if I had worked on my mindset, I could have had some important conversations and built my relationships with my family in a good way. This would have given them more opportunities to participate, all while probably shaving a year or more off the time it took to pay that debt. For you list-loving people, here is what I could have done better:

1. I could have engaged my family at a certain point and asked for their ideas on ways to spend less money but have more fun.
2. I could have expressed overall goals for finances, so everyone in my family would understand the direction I wanted to go, and why.
3. I could have made some executive decisions with con-

fidence and vision, which would have made my family more likely to be calm with any changes that were occurring as they observed my confidence and intention.

The point is not to beat ourselves up about things we did not handle perfectly in the past. We did not have that experience yet, so we made the best choice we could at the time. There is one good reason to look back at those situations, and that reason is to review your actions and the outcomes briefly, so you can draw the lesson and decide how you would revise the situation if you could have a do-over. Then, you forgive yourself and others, let it go and trust in your ability to do well next time.

CHINKS IN THE ARMOR (I DON'T NEED ARMOR)

You are not Superman, and neither am I. During extended times of stress and strain, eventually, others might notice that you are having issues. You might become volatile, distracted, depressed, or just glitch-out in your short-term memory, probably due to inability to pay attention in the moment.

I became aware that I was stuffing down a lot of emotion, and I did start to add some non-work activities to my schedule and continued those after ramping down my work schedule. I became self-aware to the point that I knew I needed to start blowing off some steam, or I was going to get volatile. When I spoke on the phone, some friends mentioned that I was sounding more depressed than normal. I also tended to respond abruptly to people. Somehow, I stumbled onto my choice to open up and try new things.

I was wound up pretty tightly, so I started doing anything that sounded remotely new, interesting or fun. I started taking tactical shooting classes. I drank a lot more often than I ever had (not on days that I was shooting though). Learning how to draw a gun from a concealed holster, fire while moving and do a fast reload while being timed requires a lot of concentration and desire to learn technique. However, there is this little thing about it...If you are threatened when you carry a weapon, there is a chance you will need to use it (again, feel free to say "duh" to that). I have no moral conflict with defending myself or my family if required, but when you are putting energy into weapons training, you have to watch yourself a bit to make sure you do not absorb or transmit any kind of trouble-seeking energy or thoughts. You have to trust yourself and spend a little time making sure your motivation for carrying a firearm is immaculate. Some people who train with firearms, and a lot of beginners for sure, talk loudly and say stupid things. If you ever have to shoot someone, it is going to change your life and you better have thought through that a bit before the situation arises, or you will be dealing with some serious stuff you did not prepare for.

I also bought a motorcycle and learned to ride that thing. Of all the activities listed above, riding a motorcycle was probably the most beneficial. While drinking and hanging out with people, you can get complacent about improving your life and just use alcohol to cope with the less satisfying aspects of your life. When riding a motorcycle, there is no internal conflict. Here is what is great about riding: I am not hurting anyone. I have to be present in the moment. It requires some skill and technique and gets more enjoyable the better you get at it. I had to build up some competence in skills that require physical and mental coordination. I had to let go of fear and trust that I would be OK riding. You take full responsibility for your situation when riding, but I never felt threatened or like a victim. Drivers around me might not be paying attention, but they have not been malicious. Ignorant or oblivious is different than mean.

I had started saying yes to new activities, having new experiences, and I met new people. I started to let go of a lot of my old beliefs about good and bad behavior and just tried to figure out what I liked again. Being around different people can help you get to know yourself better and get comfortable connecting again. Strange as it sounds, I might never have met so many cool people if I had always been living my life in a healthy balance. Some days, I sure had fun. And some days, I started to get reacquainted with myself a bit better through those interactions and new activities. As I started putting myself out there to be with new friends and do new activities, my confidence returned, and I started to pay attention to my own likes and dislikes too. As I followed my own preferences, I felt better, and there was no downside in this...

It is fine to like what you like without any other reason!

I was often distant emotionally when at home though, and I did not know how to fix that. I felt like I was running on empty at home. I think the 4 years of overwork changed me and my relationship with my family.

PEOPLE AROUND US ARE MIRRORS

Your entire life is a reflection of how you think. You cannot change yourself by altering the mirror you are looking into…you must change first, and then the reflection will change.

People you interact with reflect back and help you get to know yourself better. I have been surprised time after time how differently people I have known for years will act around or towards me, depending on how I am feeling and being. I have been in negative spiral situations with my relationships when I was habitually discontented, blaming and judging, and almost overnight had those same relationships become very peaceful and reassuring when I felt true compassion for the other person and myself. If you pay attention to how others respond to you, it can help you to identify when you are demonstrating your best qualities, and maybe some areas that could use some improvement. If you don't want to wait for people to respond to your great or terrible attitude, you could just pay attention to how you are feeling in any moment or situation. If you are feeling good and relaxed, there is a strong likelihood that you are broadcasting a good signal to people around you. If you are feeling contradiction, or confusing emotions, you might not be living that moment fully. You could be focusing on something that does not agree with what you want, and that feels bad. You could be broadcasting that uncertainty, sketchy, or negative vibe to others. If you are feeling bad in a situation, it's important to try to reach for a thought or focus that feels a little better. When you are all jumbled up, that is when things don't work out as well as they could, often just

MICHAEL BLIZMAN

because you are broadcasting anxious, confusing, or fear-based emotions to the people around you.

ENTER, THE SHADOW

It is imperative that we get to know and accept ourselves. This is necessary in order to have a full and satisfying life, and the sooner you do this, the better it is for everyone. As we shove down parts of our personalities that we do not like or are not comfortable with, those parts gain some more power over us, as we keep hiding them from others, justifying them, and trying to pretend they are not there. Carl Jung called these less desirable parts, our "shadow". These shadow parts of you are real and will eventually show themselves. And the timing of their "big reveal" is almost never ideal. The issues caused by our shadows will bleed into other areas of our lives in a lot of ways.

I have been on both the giving and receiving end of behaviors that were driven by those shadows. When you have feelings of unworthiness, fear of loss, disappointment, or shame lurking underneath, your reactions to other people might be out of whack. Without warning I have snapped cruelly at people I love, yelled and overreacted to trivial things. I have also been cut down verbally by others who were being influenced by their shadows. In all likelihood, I have been dumped or avoided by people I really liked because of their shadows too. Or maybe I did not appreciate them, and I should just own that.

Once you acknowledge your shadows, you are seeing those unappealing characteristics instead of being influenced by them, and they lose some of their power to affect you. The sooner you can see yourself fully, the sooner you will be able to manage your life better. We all can learn to accept the things about ourselves that are not necessarily aligned with what we say we value and believe.

If you ignore your shadows, they will find expression somehow and may lead you down a darker path than you need to go.

This does not necessarily mean you will be a vampire or evil person, but these shadows that you deny might make you less than honest about your motives and lead you to be duplicitous or deceitful on some level, as you try to hide things that you are ashamed of, sometimes without you being consciously aware that you are doing it.

Have you ever answered a simple question less than truthfully, and then wondered why you did that?

Something in you detected a fake threat that required a lie, and you lied. That is a shadow that is influencing you. You might be critical of people around you because you see faults in them that remind you of your own. Once you accept all of your own qualities, good and bad, the energy you used to spend hiding those will be available to follow your creative goals and you will have better results, better relationships. The shadows in your personality that you hide are not nearly as harmful as the way you are deceiving yourself and others to hide who you really are. The sooner you accept the good and bad parts of yourself, the better it will be for everyone.

When your shadows finally come into view, you might find substantial parts of yourself you would prefer not to claim...but it's still not all that bad.

Many, or maybe all of us have some ugly, gnarly aspects to our character or personalities. Most of us exaggerate how bad those parts of ourselves really are. If I had lived in either a healthy, or a less extreme way the past few years, I might have been able to continue living, completely unaware of the uglier parts of my personality. Facing this ugly side of oneself can feel destructive, painful, life-altering, life-ending, and many would understandably prefer to avoid this. My shadows are not that bad on a spectrum of possible human behaviors, but they are mine and they have affected me. Having gone through the process of discovering and accepting my shadows, I had some experiences I would not have had otherwise, and I learned.

There is no need to focus on regret or self-loathing once you have learned what you were supposed to learn and grow from it. Just take the lessons when they come and decide what you will do next. As you learn to forgive and accept yourself, you will have more compassion for yourself and for others too. This growth and having compassion for others, coupled with focusing on things that feel better to think about and taking the next right action will be reflected in how other people respond to you. When the shadow loses its grip, people start responding to you in a much friendlier way.

When you hold judgment on yourself and others, much of the world and its creatures will judge you also.

When you are compassionate to yourself, you extend compassion to others, and the entire world reflects compassion back to you in ways you could never predict.

APPROACHING THE GOAL LINE, BUT STILL NOT FEELING LIKE A WINNER

If you have any victory, it is vital to celebrate it and acknowledge your progress. As you recognize the small victories you experience, your confidence and momentum builds. Also, when you make progress, it's likely that someone helped you along the way, and that is another thing to feel grateful for. The winning pattern is to acknowledge your victory, feel gratitude for it, and look forward to your next step towards your goal. Repeat.

    One of the things that I did not do so well after so many years of working to pay off debts is to acknowledge success along the way. I had executed a plan and it worked. By the time that I completed my plan, I had been doing it a long time, and it was almost on autopilot. Also, about that time, my attention drifted to other areas of my life, and I forgot to "integrate the win" as Brendon Burchard calls it. About 2 years after most of the debts were gone, I looked at my old debt-tracking spreadsheet and realized all I had accomplished to clear those up. Then I checked my credit report and it looked a lot better too. I cared less about my finances at that point, probably because it was a less dire situation, and also because I had other concerns bubbling to the top of my mind. Still I realized that I needed to acknowledge that success, so I deliberately indulged a solid 5 minutes of sitting quietly and thinking about that situation and experiencing gratitude that it was much improved now. I was thankful for all the abilities, people, and clients that entered my life to support me in my effort to resolve that debt situation. I remember going for a walk after that and just enjoying a few more minutes of blissful thinking about this one victory. And yes, I wrote it in my journal too. After that day, I added a daily check-in with myself in the morning. During that time, I list some things I am grateful for, and I look specifically for little wins I can be grateful for.

CHANGES ARE COMING

I believe that life arranges itself in ways that lead us to whatever growth we need. About the time I scaled down my consulting work, other changes were occurring too. My employer was sold to a bigger company. I will admit that by this time, I was fully distracted by a bunch of escapist activities, just trying to feel better than I did before, any way that I could think of to try, with the exception that I did not take drugs. Like I mentioned earlier, I was still high functioning in my professional life. A couple years later, I was doing better professionally and promoted, and I was starting to crave further change and expansion in my life, and I did not look at things the same way I used to. I spent more than a year reading a lot of books, spending time thinking, talking to people, trying to find out what I might want to do, and who I might want to become. I had started to see that things I want are possible if I go after them honestly, without conflict or apology. You could say I wanted more alignment with my real self, whoever that was.

IT IS OK TO WANT WHAT YOU WANT

You have to move toward the things you want. Even if you are not quite sure what it is, if you pursue those things and adjust as you go, it will work out fine. A lot of us put our own wants on the back burner so long that we forgot what they are.

During this period, I made it a priority to value my own preferences again. I slowly began to understand that I had given away my power in the past to people who seemed to know what *they* want and were confident it was right. We all have the ability to create our life experience in ways we see fit, if we are willing to pay the price. Everyone has this ability. The price we must pay is not work or struggle in the way most of us think of such things.

To make lasting changes, the price we pay is that we must be willing to let our old identity, with all its perceived limitations die and we must take full responsibility for creating our future. And we must believe we can have a life that we want.

When I say our old identity must die, I mean that our old beliefs about our life, our old stories we tell about how we got to be how we are, the yeah-but excuses we tag onto any statement we make when we explain why we are not doing what we really want to do, and all the things you believe which might give you an excuse not to try something you really want to try.

For you list lovers, here is what you must allow to die so that you can make great changes:

    1. All your stories about yourself that justify why you are

what you are right now

2. All blaming of others for your present condition

3. All your beliefs about your limitations

4. All your excuses and yeah-buts that keep you from taking action toward what you want

We must be willing to sit with ourselves and acknowledge what we truly want with no shame or apology. We must accept and love the good and ugly parts of our nature and proceed in the direction we choose with full belief and faith that we deserve what we want, with no further reconciliation or justification, but simply because we are. We must be willing to accept all the consequences of our choices.

List-lovers, here is a list of what you must do to make great changes:

1. Acknowledge exactly what you want to experience, do, have and be, without any shame or apology

2. Accept all the awesome and ugly parts of your own character

3. Know that you deserve to have what you want, just because you are alive

4. Accept the consequences of your choices

TUNING IN TO A QUIET VOICE

There has been a lot of research and press about meditation and mindfulness over the past few years. Taking a few minutes each day for a meditation practice has been shown to improve concentration, reduce anxiety, increase happiness, and reduce negative emotions.

Over the course of this journey, I found that sitting quietly or "meditating" every morning has helped me to react less abruptly, to focus on important tasks, and at times to get in tune with something wiser than my old ego. I started having more intuition experiences and better timing and flow with others.

In 2016 when I brought up wanting a divorce, my wife was resistant to the idea and willing to discuss or try anything to save our marriage. I did not want anything to do with our marriage anymore. It held no attraction for me, even if I felt some remorse that it would hurt her and the kids. I moved to another room upstairs until April when I moved out to stay at my parents for a bit.

I had been doing a lot of work on myself mentally, emotionally and spiritually over the past eighteen months or so. One outcome of this personal work was that I developed a bit of compassion for myself and some of the clumsy ways I had been living. I had quite a number of experiences and personal challenges that forced me to change my approach to many areas of my life, but especially I had to change my way of thinking. I had some situations block certain directions I was heading, and other pathways made clear. I was noticing the difference in how those situations felt and allowing myself to be led by the emotions and the energy around those experiences. All along the way, I was doing my part to improve the quality of my own thoughts and to project a better version of me into the world, but also to leave behind some negative habits I had entertained for much of my life. As I changed the way I was thinking and being, everything around me, my relationships, and even general circumstances of the day took a positive turn.

A friend of mine, Ted, had advised me that since my soon-to-be-ex-wife and I have kids together, it would be a good use of my energy to improve that relationship or at least remove some of the venom between us. We would always be in each other's lives because of the kids, so this suggestion made sense. Without going into matters of faith or religion, I noticed that as I took steps toward being a better person, a much more intelligent higher power took steps toward me, in a reassuring way. Events, chance meetings and general "luck" occurred in ways I could never have coordinated on my own, even if I had the idea to do so, and my faith and confidence increased as a result of this experience. The experience I had around luck, meeting new people, support from all directions is a large enough topic for another chapter or even a separate book. The point for this chapter, is that I had a bit of a breakthrough in my approach to life and was experiencing some compassion for my wife and her situation, even if our interactions were still contentious at times. My wife was going through some medical issues during this time and we were texting one night after I had moved out.

One night while texting my wife, I mentioned that I knew the medical conditions were hard for her to deal with because of all the uncertainty she was feeling. She replied that at least she is certain our marriage is over.

This was the first time she had accepted that our marriage was over instead of trying to convince me to return to a marriage I did not value anymore.

When I woke up very early the next morning, I had an intuitive hit, for lack of a better way to describe it. I had a deep knowing of what I was to do. Having tuned into my own intuition, the difference could not be more obvious when comparing to the old critical inner dialog that used to dominate my mind and influence my decisions. This knowing felt full and right. That day, I asked my wife if we could meet and talk. I had a certainty that my biggest opportunity to grow as a person at that time was to attempt to relate to my wife without the hostility of the past, and to take some time to assess if there was any way to be together, given who we have become over the years.

We decided to try it. Amazingly, we were both agreeable to a primary ground rule. The main ground rule was that we would not spend time talking and digging up all the old topics about how things got screwed up, who did what first, what went wrong first or any of the other nonsense.

Why do you think I called those topics nonsense?

In my experience, it is not possible to understand all of those complex feelings and responses after even a few days have passed because,

*The person you were when those things happened
does not even exist anymore.*

A few times we have discussed some things from the past but limited those discussions to just what was needed for some understanding. Neither of us had to remind the other of our ground rule. When you dig up the past and try to untangle it, almost without variation, the only insight that might matter is generally how one of us was feeling at that moment or something that we remember wrestling with at the time, but the other person was not aware of at all. Perhaps at the time those personal issues were influencing us, we might not have been aware of them either. It was only in hindsight that we might notice some effect. It might be worth a cursory look to get context about a situation, but anything more is again, nonsense.

All of those details are in our imaginations now and are not relevant or even understandable. We are different people, with a different focus, and all that really matters is where you are now, and where you want or intend to go. Our relationship improved greatly, and much of the vitriol and venom was gone. Mostly what remained was the effort to communicate better and find out if this could work, and I think both of us grew quite a bit from this approach and experience. My wife described the approach of leaving the past alone as "freeing".

DISCOVERY

In consulting work, the "discovery" phase of a project is when the client provides a lot of information or artifacts, and the consultant gets to request a lot more information. For me, the discovery phase involved looking at my own life and beliefs, but without any need to protect or defend those things. The main thing that matters is if those beliefs are helpful or not. Once a person starts to notice things that need to change, and to de-program themselves from long-held habits of thinking which are not helpful, it may take some time to try out new things, think differently, and adjust how you approach your life.

I used to have self-critical thoughts intrude on my mind often...well, almost constantly. A lot of these were criticisms that I was not living up to some standard or belief I had always held. From about 2013 on, I started departing from much of the beliefs and behaviors that had been normal for me for so many years. This departure accelerated through 2016. As I shifted away from ways of thinking that had been my habit for most of my life, I started categorizing the thoughts I noticed as useful or not useful. If the thought led to shame or feeling powerless, it is not useful to me. It's good to recognize that we could have handled a situation better, or if our actions hurt someone; however, labeling yourself as awful or bad just makes improving yourself a lot harder, as you calling yourself something bad instead of requiring yourself to do better next time.

That is not what I want, it's not what my family or friends need from me, and if you believe in God, it's not what she wants either. All of those I mentioned want me to own my behavior, and improve so I can be better, happier, and spread more of my own energy, talent and love to others. Once I took this approach of deprogramming myself from the bullshit that I had accepted before, I found that I did not connect with the same people I used to in the same ways anymore. All my points of reference seemed to lack any meaning or familiarity, and I was drifting. People who were close to me before were pretty confused.

This is when I started looking for things that might be helpful to me in what other people did, or ideas that other belief systems extolled, or which seemed to be helpful to people before me. I read a lot of philosophy books, self-help books, listened to interviews with famous people, some not-so-famous authors, and anyone or anything that I was drawn to. I also adjusted course often. When I found that something, I was initially interested in did not connect with me anymore, I quickly dumped those things in favor of other ideas that were interesting.

I started practicing guided meditation because I heard that many people found it helpful, and it made sense as I learned more about the subject. The big point is that I tried it and noticed an improvement in my mood overall, and a drop in my "reactivity" to situations and other people after the first couple weeks of keeping just a daily 7-15-minute session.

I started trying other things deliberately to change my mood. I started going for walks and doing light stretching to make my body feel better, and to give me something to focus on. This helped to slow down my thoughts.

The people I surrounded myself with changed also. I wanted to be around people who were either upbeat, someone I aspired to be like, very supportive, or hilarious.

By leaving time for myself to seek, think and just be, I was able to make some connections I had not made before. I gave myself permission to not know everything, and time to figure it out.

I had a number of concepts or epiphanies come to me over my period of discovery which lasted about 18 months or so. These epiphanies which affected me most, are listed in the following sections.

EPIPHANY 1: IT IS RIGHT FOR ME TO BE HAPPY

During the many edits of this, I re-read between the lines of the introduction. I noticed that I would not take corrective action just for the sake of my own happiness. Instead, I had to fall down so far that I finally recognized that I soon might stop functioning well at work. I had to observe a threat to my ability to provide for my family before I would commit to any real action. This was my bottom threshold where I would take action. This is a big clue in itself to the possible root of the problem, and it took a long time and some deep reflection to recognize a core issue for me in not being interested enough in my own happiness and well-being to take action sooner or to even think about it. Worthiness and knowing we deserve to be happy is a foundational issue for many of us.

Somewhere along the way we can stop trusting our own judgement. We lose perspective about how we are supposed to decide the path we take in life based on our own preferences. We forget that we get to decide a lot of things and create our own experiences in life. We give up our power to decide for ourselves. There are probably an infinite number of reasons that we give up our power. For some of us, it's because we believe that others seem to know what to do while we do not feel certain at all about what to do. There are just as many paths to self-worth, self-love, or acceptance as there are people, but improving our life requires that we make a decision to look for our own innate value. We have to trust our own preferences. You prefer this over that, that over this. There is nothing wrong with having a preference, and every person has a unique combination of traits and preferences.

You have your preferences and you do not have to justify them to anyone.

Whenever it does not cause harm, we should follow our preferences. If you deny your preferences, you will end up living someone else's life instead of your own. If you are really honest about it, it is pretty easy to determine that you like something or not, and you do not have to defend that! Your taste is as valid as anyone else's. This quote from Steve Jobs reminds me of the value of our own preferences:

"Everything around you that you call life was made up by people that were no smarter than you and you can change it, you can influence it, you can build your own things that other people can use." –Steve Jobs

Start with this

If you have lost touch with your own preferences and just tried to serve everyone else for a long time, you can **start with** small stuff and take some time to get used to the idea. If a friend asks you where you want to go to lunch, pick a place and say you would like to go there. Even if you don't really care that much, it will demonstrate that you can express your opinion and get what you decide. Your friend will probably be relieved that you picked the place so directly and quickly and it will be a relaxing start to your lunch.

Start making little decisions quickly based on what you

prefer and follow through on those. Build the habit of expressing a preference. Tell the waiter to hold the onions instead of just picking them off yourself.

EPIPHANY 2: IT IS RIGHT TO BEGIN AS SOON AS YOU FEEL THE DESIRE

It will take some effort to correct or true-up your life to match who you really are. Many of you have a pattern of negative thoughts or self-talk and limiting beliefs. The amount of effort to change these beliefs does not change no matter *why* you decide to begin this process. But the amount of effort does increase the longer you *wait* to begin. The longer you wait to start, the harder it can become because your old mental and physical habits become stronger with time. Your surroundings and people in your life mold and form and fill in the gaps around you, much like wet concrete fills in gaps around a fence post and locks it into position. This can make it feel difficult to start a change, because you have so much that seems to be holding you in your current position. It feels like inertia, but it is not the same as inertia in physics.

Your observations tend to keep you where you are

Your life as you observe it all around you reminds you of current conditions and triggers your mind through your sight, sound, smell, etc. This kind of inertia reminds you through your senses of what is in your life today. The circumstances you see around you tend to make you feel a certain familiar way and that feeling encourages you to think and behave in the familiar ways. As you have the same thoughts and same behaviors you had *yesterday*, you will tend to experience more of those familiar events, thoughts and feelings *today*. You can break this cycle in a number of ways, so there is no excuse not to make a change if you want to. One last point on this: As soon as you feel the desire to make a change, you are ready to start, so take a step even though you do not know to where all the steps will lead.

Start with this

You can start to break the negative thought/feeling cycle in any of these ways:

1. Change your thoughts about the situation.
2. Change your physical environment.
3. Change your focus away from things that feel really bad and focus on something that is working well in your life.

Change your thoughts about the situation

When I took steps to become more aware of negative thoughts I was having, it made it easier for me to tweak those thoughts a bit. In order for me to be aware of my thoughts, I determined I needed to touch something or do something, otherwise, I would just move on without being fully aware of the thought.

Here is what I did: I carried a plastic spoon in my pocket and switched it to the other pocket of my pants every time I thought something judgmental about a certain person, then I would deliberately think of something positive, and something I am grateful for. This helped me to curb that habit of judging thoughts, and my interactions with people changed dramatically in as little time as week or so. You could use this same technique anytime you have a negative expectation or any other type of thought which might be showing up too much. This simple tactile routine in response to a troublesome thought really honed my awareness.

Tools or techniques like this can help you notice what is going on in your head, which will help you to deliberately shift your thought patterns. You are the only one who can decide what you will think. You can choose to think differently about a situation or a person. If you pay attention to your responses to situations, you might find there is an underlying story or belief that supports negative thoughts or feelings you are experiencing. If you become aware of your thoughts, you might notice patterns or things that trigger those thoughts. Once you are more aware, you can plan how to respond to those situations, or avoid them altogether for a while until you are stronger in your new habits.

Change your physical environment

Going on a trip, or just spending your free time different than normal can break up your habits too. I started hanging out to do my evening work in a different place...either a different Starbucks or a casual restaurant I had not been in before. New people to see, new noises, and a different drive home are subtle changes, but they help. If you leave where you currently are, much of the old stimuli will not be around and current observations will be removed from your daily life. Without these reminders, you will not have the same things triggering your habitual thoughts and actions anymore and it can be easier to set your attention and thoughts on a new path. Sometimes changing your environment is the right thing to do.

A word of caution about this option though--Taking it to the extreme might be "the nuclear option" and quite destructive to your existing life, which may or may not be appropriate for you. Not everyone is willing to or able to change their environment. For example, if you are living in a house with a mortgage, with a spouse you do not get along with lately but have children you like living with, you might not want to leave the home or you might not be financially able to move out. You may want to explore other less destructive ways to break the cycle first, if for no other reason, simply so you have some inner peace if you later choose the "nuclear option".

Change your focus

Change your focus away from things that feel really bad and focus on something that is working well in your life.

Writing in my journal about things that I am grateful for really helped a lot. Asking myself what is good about a situation, even in a negative situation, also helped me learn this. If you keep mulling over your big problem and how bad it feels, you are not likely to come up with any solution. You are just going to feel bad if you do that. When you feel bad, you have bad ideas. Get into a better mood first by thinking about something that is going well or that you are grateful for. As you do that, the problem areas of your life often start to improve on their own without any special effort from you. I cannot explain why this happens, but I have observed and experienced it.

A common thread

Did you notice that all three of the items above started with the word, "change"? Do something different...anything different if you do not have a great idea but start now. There is a reason to start your journey now. If you are ignoring that you are not feeling good about your life, you are sleepwalking through your days. As you are sleepwalking through life, everything around you is changing. The longer you wait, the more likely it is that you are adding risk of losing your important relationships, potential relationships, and new opportunities that you cannot see while in this fog. No matter where you are in life right now, the sooner you can begin to wake up and start moving toward a life you choose, the better it will be for everyone involved, including yourself.

I feel like I should balance the previous sentences. A call to action is appropriate and beneficial to recognize and respond to problems in life sooner rather than later. However, there is no fake urgency here to do something right now. Acting rashly or while motivated from fear is not usually a good way start. Fear is a terrible thing to feel, and the ideas you have while in fear are usually not the greatest. While in anger, you might not be coming up with optimal solutions, you are in a probably in a slightly better place than fear. Anger prompts you to do something to put a stop to something you do not like, while fear tends to stall us from taking any action.

Knowing you have a problem to deal with is a good start and working on yourself, so you will be taking action out of love and faith will yield more pleasant outcomes usually, if you can do it. As you become a better version of yourself, the people in your life will adapt. The sooner you show yourself, the sooner your real relationships will bloom, or end and be replaced with better-fitting relationships. People adapting to you is not always pleasant. Sometimes they realize they don't want to be around you, or vice versa. The sooner you start, the sooner you will regain time and energy as the people and situations who do not suit you become less prominent in your life...you will have more time and energy to spend on things you really like.

Beliefs are persistent, habitual thoughts. You can alter your thoughts and beliefs. You can shift your thought habits toward things that serve you better. If you believe you are powerless to change something, you might feel quite frustrated and depressed, and you will not try to change it. If you believe you *can* change something, you *will* come up with ways to approach the problem until something works. If you believe that someone is doing the best they can, you might have some compassion for them. Beliefs are not absolutely true, but are stories formed when you perceive something or someone, based on how you interpreted events in the past. They are true for you. You can adjust or change those beliefs, and this will change how you see things. Your beliefs will also change the way people respond to *you*, because your feelings are felt by other people around you-people pick up your attitude or vibe.

If you are open to simply doing something different so that you can feel better than you do today, you can get on a path of discovering your own value and changing how you look at the world. You can find a way to remember who you are and to move toward becoming the best version of yourself.

EPIPHANY 3: I AM COMPLETELY RESPONSIBLE FOR MY LIFE

At a certain point, I realized that the common thread running through most of the books I had read is that I am responsible for everything I experience in my life. Either this is absolutely true, or the belief that it is true is the most empowering option and therefore the most helpful personal philosophy. So based on this premise, I choose to believe the following statements.

- Every single thing I am experiencing today is because of a decision I made, or a decision I did not make, a thought I had, or a judgement I made.

- Even when seemingly random events occur in my life, my response to those events and how I think about them determine what my experience will be in the next moments.

- Through my judgements, I have tuned out or blocked many people and experiences from my life.

There are things we can change and things we cannot. It is useless to ponder the things we cannot change for much longer than the time necessary to recognize them as such. None of us can change the decisions we have made or did not make, or the things we have done and said. The only thing you can influence is what you do next. What you do next and how you feel in any moment is determined by how you think. And you are the only person who can control what you think.

It is not always easy to control what you think about, but you can practice ways to get better at this. Before describing how to direct your thoughts, this is why our thoughts matter.

Through our thoughts, we imagine and expect outcomes and responses from others. Our mind wants to be right. Our expectations influence how we interact with others, and often become self-fulfilling prophecies. At a minimum our thoughts create an environment that matches and supports a *level* or type of outcome that is similar to our thoughts and expectations.

Our minds want to be right

Our expectations lead us to look for evidence to support those expectations. This is often called confirmation bias, but this term sounds very clinical, and obscures the effect it has in creating a life of excitement and abundance, or of fear and lack, depending upon the nature of our thoughts and expectations. The point is that it is not likely that we will have a great outcome when we are afraid or feeling lousy. The most reliable method to become afraid or to feel bad is to imagine or expect bad things to happen. If you are focused on the things you hate about your job or your mate, it is not likely that those things are going to suddenly get better. If you focus on what you appreciate about those things and people, you have a better chance of seeing improvements.

EPIPHANY 4: FEELING BETTER IS THE MAIN THING I CAN DO

Feeling better is the best thing I can do for me and those around me.

When we are feeling really bad, it is hard to change direction quickly toward feeling great. How many times do you see someone move from a job they hate and are miserable in immediately to their dream job? It's not very often. How often do you see a person go from a bad relationship right into a great relationship? Isn't it more common to see your friend in a bad situation, and then the job or the name and face of their significant other might change, but the situation is mostly still the same? Most of us have that friend who is still in a pseudo-non-relationship but with a different person than a year ago. Or the friend whose job still is about the same...the new boss has a different name, but the situation is mostly the same as before.

When the trash is falling down on you, going to the perfect situation might not be feasible. Instead, you might have to take a baby-step in the right direction or go to neutral first. If you are in a job you hate, you might have to find a way to get "OK" with it or find something good about it to focus on before you find a better job. If you are in a bad relationship, you might want to either break up and spend some time alone to get yourself right, or find something to appreciate about your current situation, while you decide what you want.

I know this sounds like a mind-game you're playing with yourself, and it is. It is also how people find happiness, make positive changes, and find meaning in their lives. It's all an inside job.

Remember that the fastest way to feel better is to focus on something in your life that is going well, or you are encouraged by because it might go well. Get your mind off of the thing that is making you feel terrible.

EPIPHANY 5: MY THOUGHTS DETERMINE HOW I EXPERIENCE LIFE

My thoughts and perceptions determine how I experience life . As an example, consider a trip from Atlanta to Houston recently. I was on a routine trip I took for work. It is only a two-hour trip, so it's no big deal. Just a couple rows in front of me sat a lady who was tense and appeared quite sure the plane was going to crash. Let me ask you, what kind of experience is that person having? If you were to talk to this person while flying, their tension and fear will color most aspects of the conversation. Even if they do not directly talk about their fear, you will pick up on the vibration they are giving off, and you may feel tense around them. The man in the seat next to me was quite relaxed, friendly but not too talkative. It was easy for me to enjoy the flight because he was relaxed. We had a short conversation while beverages were handed out by the flight attendants, and then I went back to listening to an audio book, and he went back to watching his movie. All 3 of us were on the same flight, but me and the guy next to me had a pleasant and relaxed experience, while the lady a few rows up was tense and probably making those around her tense too. Any way you look at it, the calm person is going to have a more pleasant flight than the person with anxiety will have. And so is the person sitting next to a calm person.

MICHAEL BLIZMAN

Every person around us is affected by how we are feeling

Every person that comes into contact with us is likely to be affected by our expectations about the flight. A nervous traveler can make the people around them tense. And a happy traveler can influence others around them too. It's the same flight, almost the same seat, but two different types of thoughts in the mind of the person in the seat. One person is experiencing fear, and the other is having a wonderful trip. Our thoughts determine our experience. Our thoughts affect the experiences of those around us too.

*Judgements, expectations and beliefs
are all types of thoughts*

My thoughts make me feel a certain way. Those thoughts and feelings lead to situations that line up with those thoughts and feelings. If things are going less-than-great, it is hard to accept that I am the one who creates most of that situation...but with acceptance of this comes the realization that I have the power to change all of it too. Because of this one fact, I am able to change every aspect of my life:

I control what I think, no one else

While it is true you are the only one who can control what you think, that does not mean it comes naturally or is easy to do all the time.

*I had no idea how to stop thinking about something,
even if it was not helping me*

I do not know of any standard part of the educational system that instructs students how to interrupt a thought that is not helpful, or about controlling one's focus. In Western society, these skills might come to a person as a by-product of a religious or spiritual practice but are not a primary focus. I saw a need in myself for this skill, and I sought a way to gain this ability.

First, I tried to not think about the thing that was bothering me. That did not work. Try it yourself: Do not think about a red train, or a pink horse. The more you resist a thought, the stronger it gets. When troublesome thoughts are invading, what seems to help most is if I don't resist or judge those thoughts, but just let them pass through on their own. Or take a nap. Eventually, I started to learn more about meditation because it helps me put my mind in neutral, which gives some space for better thoughts to arrive. So, this epiphany led to at least one of the practices I adopted, meditation, which is described in the "What Works" section of this book.

Feeling better will tend to bring you together with people and situations that also feel better to be with. As people and situations in your circle improve, you will be supported by those around you and they will pull you up further. In the other direction people and situations that do not line up with your more positive ways will fall away and lose prominence in your life and in your thoughts over time. Useless thoughts will starve for lack of attention because you are interested in new things that you are choosing to focus on. You are controlling your focus. Those negative things that you used to think about all the time will lose relative importance as the world around you changes…as new people and situations start to show up.

THE PAGE TURNS AND EMOTIONS SUCK

Emotions don't actually suck, but they can feel good and can feel bad. Feelings are helpful in a few ways. First, emotions such as anger or frustration can fuel us to focus our energy and effort on something specific that we want to change and help us get more dramatic results. Second, emotions indicate if we are on track or not.

A positive emotion indicates when we are set up favorably to win at something we are focusing on. Feeling good means that you have a desire for something, and you believe you can do it or achieve it...like you are heading for a win. Sometimes we have a desire but doubt we can have it fulfilled, and that feels terrible. There is a balance to achieve when confronted with problems. On one hand, focusing on the problem locks in our thinking and often blocks us from finding a solution. On the other hand, ignoring things that bother you often lets the problem grow. Ignoring your negative feeling emotions and what is causing them is that the problems you are ignoring seem to just keep getting bigger until you are willing to notice them and pay some attention to them.

A negative emotion most often indicates when we are not lined up with our best selves. If you are not accepting something or resisting something that has occurred and are feeling terrible, that generally does not help you. Our best selves can aim for the best outcome in any situation, and flex from previous expectations when appropriate. Feeling bad usually means you are not behaving in a way that aligns with your truest beliefs and values, and we are not heading naturally to what most would call success.

Until we acknowledge what we really feel, those feelings will grow until they overflow to affect many parts of your life

I believe this is just the way we are made. The way I look at it now is this: The fact that our unresolved problems keep getting bigger and heavier in our lives until we deal with them demonstrates that God or whatever you believe created us, loves us...loves us enough to make sure we acquire a desire strong enough for us to eventually deal with our issues and grow past our current limitations. We can leave old weaknesses behind.

Unresolved problems and emotions keep growing louder and louder until we acknowledge them, and probably until we deal with and outgrow them. Left unresolved, these circumstances represent weakness.

Weaknesses are not something we can run away from, but something we leave behind by making decisions.

ARE YOU STUCK?

The cognitive triangle:

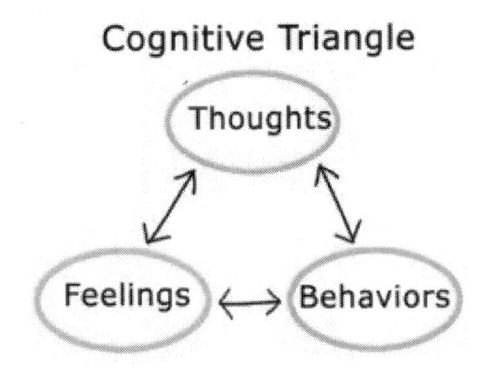

Cognitive Triangle

```
         Thoughts
          ↗  ↖
         ↙    ↘
   Feelings ←→ Behaviors
```

This cycle will tend to keep us "stuck" in familiar circumstances or patterns. Our persistent thoughts, resistance to changing circumstance, and perceived limitations lead to specific emotions and behaviors. Those emotions and behaviors filter our perceptions to support what we are thinking, feeling, and believing. In fact, we will always find evidence to reinforce our thoughts, emotions, and behaviors. You are not really "stuck" by the way. You are recreating the same pattern by selecting the same experience through your habitual thoughts and emotions each day. You could interrupt the pattern by changing your thoughts.

A lot of times, you might notice that there is some pattern that keeps showing up in your life. Some examples of a pattern might be: A certain point in your relationships you cannot seem to get past, a career ceiling, or some behavior that keeps you from going forward in certain situations. Where do you shut down or stop? A lot of people have repeating patterns in their lives and they all lead to this point where they just stop making progress toward their goal...this is your area of resistance. This point, issue or pattern is the very thing that points to what you need to work on! This is what needs attention and you will keep hitting the same experiences or limits until you are ready to leave it behind by facing your discomfort, or otherwise growing enough to get to another area of resistance.

When you hit these points, the most direct way to break the cycle is to change your thought first. To change your thoughts, ask yourself better questions like these:

- "What would it feel like if what I want to happen actually happens?"
- "What might be good about this?"
- "What am I to learn from this?"
- "What is being drawn from me?"
- "What must I become to move past this?"

Your mind is designed to work on questions and problems you assign to it. As your mind tries to answer those questions, you will experience an emotion that corresponds with those thoughts, and those thoughts and feelings will affect the way you interact with the people and situations around you.

Pay some attention to the thoughts and feelings you experience before and when you hit a bump in your life. Then ask better questions when you talk to yourself and note how your reactions and behaviors to events and people around you smooth out a bit.

YOU KNOW WHAT YOUR PROBLEM IS?

For quite some time, I have had this edgy vision in my head of a coach or mentor starting a session by asking the question, "You know what your problem is?" (Color the question with a tough New York accent to get the full effect). I guess this is attractive to me because the tone is completely unexpected from and unfitting from a therapist but might be OK from a coach.

IT'S SERIOUS, BUT NOT THAT SERIOUS

While I appreciate some gentleness when speaking with others, sometimes we are way too soft in how we approach communication. Sometimes a conversation ends, and I am not even clear about what the other person was trying to say. It as if we are so focused on not making ourselves or the other person uncomfortable, that the purpose of speaking to one another is secondary or altogether lost. Maybe this is a by-product of the conditioning from office or school environments we spent a lot of time in, or not wanting to be uncomfortable ourselves, or to make others uncomfortable.

I am not sure what the cause, but I like the idea of approaching someone with some in-your-face contrast, and with a bit of love and humor as well. This way, it signals that while important enough to address, the problems they are experiencing are not so terrible that we cannot rise above them and laugh a bit along the way. The other part of this is that if someone can still connect and laugh when we have this kind of approach, I have no doubt that we can get to know each other and work on something together while having a good time, most of the time. Some people may think I am not taking the big talks and problems seriously enough. I respectfully disagree. I will try to be respectful of how they receive my words, but I know that being ultra-serious about a BIG problem does not often lead to quick resolution of the problem...the solution usually occurs later, after most of the drama or intensity has lightened up and we are somewhat relaxed. Usually while in the shower or waking up from nap. The solution would

MICHAEL BLIZMAN

present itself much sooner if we could not take the problem so damned seriously for so long.

LOOK FOR PATTERNS FIRST

So, do you know what your problem is? Instead of going right into all the specifics and listing out horrible things and feelings, stay general and list out the broad strokes first. You can paint in the details later as needed. Is it your relationships? Is it your finances? Your anxious thoughts? What is it that is keeping you from launching toward that thing you dream about? Do you have some idea of what the underlying causes might be for your big issue? Or are you not sure yet?

If you are down about your relationships, is it just one relationship, or is it all of your relationships? Sometimes we are very aware of a problem with our significant other relationship because that relationship is really in your face and obvious because of all the different aspects wrapped up in that relationship. In addition to just getting along with the person, with your mate, you might have shared finances, children, intimacy and other dimensions that are really loaded with enormous personal investment, potential conflict, and emotion. But is that the only relationship that features a negative feeling with it, or is there a thread common to all your relationships that you have not identified? I am not recommending any self-loathing here, but if you take some quiet time to reflect, do you have a hard time expressing yourself with your other friends? Your children? Your parents? How cut-off from people are you? If you notice something common to all or many of your relationships, it is hard to come to the conclusion that your problems are because your mom is cold, or your spouse is a jackass. It is more likely there is an issue in yourself you need to acknowledge and resolve. If you have a problem with everyone, the problem is likely you. Once you accept that the "problem" is your behavior or attitude, it is possible to drill into that a bit more precisely, so you can determine next steps.

Are you down about your finances? Is this a recent occurrence for you, or have you had financial challenges your entire life? What kind of problems are you having? For example, do you seem stuck at a certain income level and are not able to get promoted above it? Or do you keep getting raises but are just getting further into debt with each increase in your income? Do you have a big entanglement with credit cards, or do you like fancy cars that you cannot afford?

Or are you having a career issue? Are you feeling stuck or not sure about what you should do next? Have you been fired from your last 3 jobs? Did you get passed up for a promotion…again?

I am not suggesting you analyze everything in your life deeply yet. First you should be honest about what kind of problems are *showing up* in your life. List your major issues or concerns generally at first. Then look for patterns and root causes later.

> *If you jump into solving for root cause too early, you might be missing some pattern, or not be able to see the root cause or tendency that is affecting **multiple** areas of your life*

As a basic example or hint, it is possible that a person could have a deep belief or habitual thought that makes it more likely that more than one area of their life will be troublesome. They might have a pattern of thought that makes it unlikely they will keep a long-term relationship and blocks them from higher achievement in their career at the same time. I have noticed some overlap with people who experience a weight problem, excessive debt, and clutter in their spaces. It's not always this way, but it is important to notice the areas you are dissatisfied with, and then look for patterns or thoughts that lead to those. If there is a correlation, when you change the belief that is causing one of the problems, the other areas will get some lift too. If you have more than one big problem area going on, it would be a great idea to do some self-examination to figure out if there is a single cause or belief driving all the signs showing up in your life. Often, adjusting just one belief or pattern of thought could elevate several areas of your life!

INTEGRATION VERSUS DIVIDE AND CONQUER

As a software developer, I often use the "divide and conquer" approach to break big problems into smaller ones that are relatively simple to fix. By doing this, I solve little problems one by one, and show consistent progress on a path I have defined. This makes me happy. Tony Robbins makes a great point that we are most happy when we are making progress.

This divide and conquer approach works great for resolving specific issues. With complex projects like a big software product, or maybe a different type of project described as "satisfaction in your life", for example, there is another step that we must also complete in order to be successful. For a really high-quality overall outcome, we always have to integrate those small solutions into the whole. In software development, there is an integration test and even a full end-to-end test of a process to make sure the problems we targeted are indeed solved, and that we have not introduced a new unexpected problem with the changes we have made. In addition, a truly great product will have a consistency in the feel and flow experienced while using the product. This is because all of the individual features of the product match a vision or overarching principle or vision of the product owner/creator. The features are consistent. For example, consider the iPhone. It was awesome when you first used it: it was visually attractive, easy to use, and felt good in your hand. The whole user experience was consistent with a vision for that product. Imagine how different the iPhone would have been if it required a stylus to type on it, or if it was a lot lighter and made of cheap plastic. Despite the other features remaining identical, the character and end result of the product would have been very different.

In personal development, it is important to show progress in the areas of your life that concern you, but it is also important to look at your whole self to make sure you are moving toward general well-being

When you skip that big integration step, you might solve a specific problem in your life by losing 20 pounds, but if the underlying cause of that is still around, you might gain the weight back and then some. If the underlying thought or belief persists, you might have lost weight, but the pattern will show its effects in other areas like your relationships or finances.

People are the ultimate example of a complex system

Our minds are complicated, our experiences are diverse, and we are banging around this world with other complex people who are not in optimal condition and respond to us in ways that appear erratic.

One way to add to our well-being is to do some regular practices that support it. Some of the things that helped me are in the "What Works" section later in this book.

ACKNOWLEDGE SMALL VICTORIES

In addition to good routines and habits that help you to feel well, another way to add to your well-being is to deliberately acknowledge your victories along the way. If you lose 5 pounds, acknowledge that you did that and be grateful you have that ability. It's true, and it feels good. If you paid off a debt or earned a promotion or whatever it is, acknowledge that you kicked some butt and be grateful for that win. If you kind of wanted another one-night-stand or to have way too much to drink tonight, but opted out this time, you changed your default behavior. Tell a friend, write down your success in a journal, but do something to recognize that you won a contest. You set a goal, worked your tail off or changed your approach, changed your thinking, made a decision or changed your world in some way. Celebrating when you have a win reminds you that you are powerful enough to change things to better fit how you want them to be. When you recognize your own power, it helps you to look for other things to improve and make them the way you prefer them.

HOW LONG CAN YOU TAKE TO SOLVE YOUR BIG PROBLEM?

From my experience, any mature adult should be able to deal with a problem such as debt or other issues which can be corrected in known ways and work a plan to fix that over a two or two-and-a-half-year period at the most. As a recovering superhero (yeah right), I now realize that keeping my excessive work schedule for four years was way too much. In my estimation, after 30 months, that work schedule will change a person. The excessive work schedule will change even the most stoic person more than that effort they are putting out will change the problem they are trying to fix. This is similar to what an economist might label as "diminishing marginal returns" for the time invested, but with people, it's a bit worse than that. The experience of staying out of balance to focus on one thing while ignoring most other aspects of one's life and wellbeing changes the way a person behaves, what they believe, how they think, and limits the fun things that make for interesting relationships with other people.

If you commit to some big goal like paying off some debt, you can do that for two years or so. After the goal is achieved, you can then exit from the extra activities with a short period of adjustment time, and be who you are, albeit a more grown up version of yourself. If, however, you are doing anything regularly for more than 30 months, we are not talking about a simple habit anymore or a mid-range, temporary goal. We are talking about a lifestyle. Lifestyles alter what you experience, what you believe, how your body looks and functions, and your relationships. If you stay like I did for 4 years in a self-inflicted high stress lifestyle focused on work, you will appear to be a different person at the end of it. You could experience a similar type of change if you stay in a heavily conflicted relationship for a long time. I imagine that about 2 and a half years of that would be the limit for most people to work through whatever situation they needed to. If that relationship were to drag on in an unresolved way for another year or so, both people would likely change a lot, and not necessarily in a healthy way. There would be feelings of lack of growth, self-deception, damaged self-esteem because you might forget that you deserve something better in your life, etc.

> *There is a path forward from this self-inflicted damage, but you might not resemble that person you used to be to those you are closest to when you emerge from it.*

It is as if you went on a long trip and then came back. In that time, you have changed, the people you were apart from changed too. You will have to get used to each other again if you are going to be around each other. I am not saying it is bad or good, but I will say it is risky to go so far out of balance for more than 2 years. Some people spend the rest of their lives in some crazy stress mode because they get stuck in that lifestyle. A more balanced approach to life might help you grow in concert with the people you are closest to and avoid some of the more the drastic changes.

WHAT IS HOLDING YOU BACK?

If it takes you more than two and a half years to make a significant change, it is possible that you might be strongly affected by one or more of the attributes that basically limit your progress. Most people experience some or all of these at different times in their lives, but if you recognize them here and do not try to move past them, you might be a bit crazy. Do these characteristics describe you?

- Concerned too much what others think
- Unsure of what you want
- Conflicted (that thing I want to experience would be great, but....)
- Uncommitted or lacking focus

Concerned What Others Think

I could have downsized our home to cut expenses, or cancelled cable television immediately in order to shorten the amount of time it took to clear up those old debts. I could have insisted on cutting out extracurricular activities to reduce expenditures too, but I did not want others to think less of me, or for my kids to feel like they were missing out on something. I did not want other people to know my real situation or that I was not doing well financially. It seemed like other people had it all worked out and to be thriving financially, and I did not want other people to think less of me for my lack of achievement in the financial arena.

A couple of thoughts occurred to me about this. I have come to know since this period in my life that many of those people who seemed to be thriving and having all the outward signs of wealth, are nothing close to what I would describe as wealthy or abundant. A lot of those individuals and families are working 2 jobs they hate, are in debt up to their ears, and are barely making it, even if they drive a really nice car. I do not say this to judge, but only to point out that your perceptions when you are in a down-looking phase of your life usually are not how things really are.

Our perceptions of everything around us are colored by our beliefs, our emotional state, and anything we think about regularly.

When you are struggling in some area, you might mistakenly believe that everyone else has their stuff together. Once you raise your level a little bit, you will start to notice that what you believed about those people once is not necessarily true. Your awareness will increase. Truly prosperous people do not look down on others who are in the middle of correcting a financial aspect of their life. Most people who are prospering financially went through a time of adjustment and planning to get where they are today. A prosperous person would never point out that your car is 15 years old because they know it doesn't really matter. You might even want to adopt a belief that those prosperous folks you see around you are silently rooting for you to handle your finances appropriately, so you can also live well, even if it takes some time for you to work out the details. Another belief you might consider is that most prosperous people do not think about your money situation at all and do not think about finances the way you do when you have been struggling.

Unsure of what you want

Not knowing what you want is very common. We often discount what we want in favor of what others want. We can do this so much that we forget that we actually do have a preference and it is right for us to have such preferences. Our preferences guide us through our path in life if we pay attention to them (See Epiphany 1: It is right for me to be happy). Spend some quiet time every day and try some of the other practices in this book to help you get back in touch with what you really want.

Conflicted

You could have an internal conflict because you think that what you want is opposed to some belief and value you hold in relation to the situation you are in. If finances are the issue in front of you and it is taking more than 2 years to resolve, you may be unwilling to lower your lifestyle temporarily. For me, I felt like if I reduced our lifestyle even temporarily, I was punishing my kids for my failure to manage my finances. This conflicted strongly with my self-image as a man, as a dad...you get the picture, it was a heavy load and I would not release that load easily. So, I opted to work longer and harder instead, trying to be Superman. In hindsight, my family would have been fine and totally supportive if I asked for ways to cut expenses...I did not need to bear the burden all myself. Here is my suggestion: Get over it and have some respect for yourself. Ask for what you need instead of running yourself into the ground.

Here are some examples of how this conflict shows up in relationships. If the problem is a lingering relationship problem with your spouse or significant other, you might have a conflict in that you do not believe you have the power to fix the situation, and that a lot of bad things will happen if you break up. As a result, you stay in an unfulfilling situation way too long and take little or no action to improve things. Or you might not be able to take the next step toward a committed relationship because you do not believe it will work out, or other bad things will happen if you pursue the relationship wholeheartedly. This can be some deep-seated belief that you are not good at relationships, that you are unworthy, or something like that.

Uncommitted or lacking focus

If you are paying down debt as your main goal, you can either make more money, you can reduce your spending, reallocate your spending, or a mix of these. I focused on making more money to pay off the debt, and I cut some expenditures, but we could have cut many, many more expenses to shave off the time it took to eliminate the debt.

Here is where the uncommitted part comes in. Imagine this scenario: If you were trying to reduce debt by cutting expenses only, and it was something only your significant other wanted you to do, you might not be as dedicated to the goal as you would be if you came to the decision on your own. Same thing with diet and exercise...if the doctor tells you to lose weight and eat vegetables, you might just ignore all of it. On the other hand, if you are starting to date again after a long-term relationship breaks up, you might jump wholeheartedly into a diet and exercise program with full commitment because you want to be as attractive as possible, believing that this will give you more options. After you find a good dating prospect, you might stay motivated so that you can look good naked when that time arrives. The bottom line is that the thing you say you are trying to accomplish has to be important and meaningful to you, or your interest will fade.

If it's important, you will find a way, if it's not important, you will find an excuse. -Ryan Blair

ONE SOURCE OF TROUBLES - I SHOULD...

The pattern of doing what we think we should do, instead of actively and responsibly building a good life, with friends, fun, and lucrative work, is very common.

I am not necessarily suggesting that you should ignore responsibilities and go do whatever you feel like. But sometimes we cling too much to our idea of duty and responsibility, and it would not hurt anything if you took a small break from those things and did something you really want to do.

There are plenty of times when I have finally given myself permission to take a break from something I was doing, and I ended up having a really fun time, or meeting someone that became a business contact or even a good friend, or I learned something new that helped me in ways I could not have predicted. Sometimes your intuition is telling you to get out of your rut and do that cool thing. When you get back to your routine, you might be relaxed and more able to see a solution to some problem because you are seeing it with fresh eyes and are energized again.

I do not have one single example of something perfect and awesome presenting itself when I was grouchy, tired, and frustrated. The awesome stuff happens when you are in a flow, relaxed or having fun, and often when you are happily collaborating with others, or sometimes just calm and accepting what is in the moment.

If you are totally locked into what you *should* do instead of what you *want* to do, then read this:

Start scheduling time for activities you enjoy and downtime away from your normal work to refresh your spirit and enjoy your life a bit.

You will get more done this way, and you will have more fun. You should value fun for its own sake.

ANOTHER SOURCE OF TROUBLE - OUR THOUGHTS

If you are dealing with a loss or very stressful situation, the only thing you can absolutely control is what you think about that thing. Nobody else can control your thoughts. Your thoughts create how you feel.

If you lost a job, you can either continue thinking about "...what those bastards did to you..." and try finding a new job while you are still feeling like a victim, or you can figure out what you want to do next, how the experience at your last job helped you to grow, and then seek a new job from a position of excitement and growth. You get to take some control over what happens next.

If you are heading toward a break-up or a divorce, you are probably feeling bad almost every time you interact with that person. Getting past this period of feeling bad with every interaction or reliving past events with your partner that are upsetting is going to require a lot of change on your part. There is nothing you can do to change the other person. It's all you baby! This is especially true if you plan to stay with your partner. If you end up separated, you will not have the daily interactions and potential re-triggering of those old emotions and patterns. If you have children or other reason to continue seeing each other after a breakup, you might want to learn to stop triggering and hurting each other, since you are going to have this person in your life for a

MICHAEL BLIZMAN

very long time. You might as well make it as peaceful for yourself as you can.

The most effective way I know to change what you experience is to change the way you think

WHAT IS A THOUGHT?

A thought is a memory or imagined event or idea. Thoughts are either memories of past events, or our imaginations showing us what could happen in the future, or perhaps what you would do if you could relive a moment. In any case, the thought you are having will result in a feeling, just as if you were experiencing the actual event at that moment. People are unique in this ability to relive a moment and all its accompanying emotion over and over again through imagination. While a rabbit being chased by a dog will be highly stressed while the chase is happening, if he survives the chase, the rabbit will be back to normal in few minutes. A person who has the same experience as the rabbit, however, is likely to relive being chased by a dog with all the physical effects over and over again as he remembers it in detail and feels all the emotions in response to the memory. He will experience a fight or flight response every time they recount the story for sympathetic friends, or remembers the experience to themselves while stuck in traffic, etc. The same is true for imagining being chased in the future. That imaginary event will trigger the same emotion, heart rate increase and adrenaline dump as the actual chase did. And we can run these thoughts in our heads over and over. We people are amazing. Once I realized this way our memories work, my next question was this: What exactly is my mind trying to do?

WHAT IS YOUR MIND TRYING TO DO?

Your mind is trying to keep you safe. It is not trying to make you happy.

Survival has been its main motivator for thousands of years, whereas happiness is a rather recent goal. In modern life, most daily threats to our survival have been tempered. If there are no threats to survival, the mind as most of us know it, would have no purpose. It seems like for most of us, our minds treat a number of non-fatal situations as if they will cause death, rather than just being unfamiliar, or causing discomfort or embarrassment. Some of the physical changes that happen with thoughts or an actual threatening experience, include release of chemicals our bodies produce, such as adrenaline, dopamine, or endorphins for example. Consider how the possibility of experiencing any of the things below will likely trigger a fight or flight response in many people:

1. Public speaking

2. Significant other breaks up with us

3. We make a mistake that others notice

4. Job loss

5. A poor grade in calculus

6. Anticipation or memory of any of the above, or about a million other possibilities

THOUGHTS YOU HAVE OFTEN, FORM BELIEFS

If you hear, imagine or think something over and over again, you are likely to believe it is true. This is especially the case with our own negative thoughts! Just because they are thoughts in our minds, we tend to believe them more than we should. We actually believe those thoughts are us. What I have since realized is that our thoughts are mostly just interpretations of what we experience at a point in time, coupled with the beliefs that we hold. Beliefs color our perceptions

The beliefs we hold filter and color how we perceive things too. We really cannot see things as they actually are but tend to see things in a way that supports the beliefs, we already have...we prove ourselves right every chance we get. Those repetitive thoughts often trigger emotions and they create or reinforce existing beliefs which may or may not be helpful or objectively true. The interesting thing about people is that we have the unique ability to experience an event as if it is happening, just by imagining it or remembering it.

If the rabbit I mentioned earlier escapes from a dog that is chasing it, ten minutes later the rabbit is fine and eating some lettuce. A person will likely remember being chased over and over, reliving the chase and all the fear and tension again. Each time we remember, we relive that moment and have the same adrenalin dump during the remembrance that they had during the actual chase. We can do this hundreds of times a day. The frequency of the memory combined with the emotional charge can make the event seem much more significant than it deserves to be. That event happened, but so what? It is our response to the event that determines the importance of the event.

> *"...for there is nothing either good or bad, but thinking makes it so..."* --Hamlet, William Shakespeare

THOUGHTS ARE ADDICTIVE

If a person can get addicted to dopamine releases and endorphins and other chemicals produced in the body, and if our thoughts can cause our bodies to produce these chemicals repeatedly and predictably, then do you think it is reasonable that a thought which triggers a chemical response might tend to become a pattern and even become addictive to us? Dr. Joe Dispensa has a large and excellent body of work on this topic if you would like to dive into more details.

We get addicted to our own repetitive thoughts.

As we have negative thoughts about all the bad things that might happen, the chemicals released create feelings to which we become accustomed. They are familiar. The same effect happens when we have positive thoughts repeatedly, but the chemicals and feelings produced by positive thoughts are different. If you have been primarily negative for a long time, switching to a more positive mindset could to throw your system out of whack for a while, until the adjustment is made in all downstream systems and receptors. You might experience discomfort or even symptoms of withdrawal when you start throttling down your experiences of anger, frustration, and of generally expecting the worst from people. Being at peace or happy is going to feel strange for a while too. If you are very negative, trying to move toward very positive quickly could be quite shocking and your mind will pull out a lot of tricks to get you to stay the way you have been--it is familiar and comfortable for the mind to stay as it is, and to the mind, anything unfamiliar means death could be near.

> *"People will choose unhappiness over uncertainty."*
> *–Tim Ferris*

Your mind likes things the way they are. After you start to improve your thought-habits, you are likely to notice a shift that feels great after a short time. But it is totally normal to get sucked back into the old ways of thinking, to discount that the changes you are making are really helpful, and to doubt that you will be able to get the results you are wanting for the long term. The old you will express itself as an inner critic or similar voice to try to pull you back to the familiar old patterns. You will find yourself thinking about old situations and how those things felt bad for no reason sometimes. Your old inner voice may even berate you and call you hopeless because you cannot prevent the old negative thoughts from popping back up sometimes. Do not believe this thought! You can observe a thought without feeling all the same emotions that used to accompany it. You can notice the thought, acknowledge it as interesting, and then choose to focus on your breath, or distract yourself with another thought that feels better.

With practice, you can get to a point where you notice and observe that these old thoughts have popped up, without making them super-important. As long as you do not believe your thoughts automatically as they arrive, you are doing well. And you can continue your path to a better way of living.

THOUGHTS ARE HYPERLINKED

Here is another interesting thing to consider. Memory seems to be dynamic, not like something carved in a stone tablet like we might expect. Every time we remember something, we add a little bit of context to that memory from our current situation or a reference to what we are experiencing in the current moment. These new additions to the old memories increase the chance that another experience will trigger the memory, because the new additions are extra associations that can link to that memory. It is like the "telephone game" for the thoughts in your head, or new hyperlinks on websites that link back to the original page. One memory causes another memory to be recalled, but this memory gets altered just a little bit each time it is repeated based on the current situation! Over time, our memories can get skewed, blurred, and become very strange departures from what the original memory was. As you stew about something for a long time, the triggers for that memory spider web out and get linked to other things. It is important to manage this stewing and extra associations ASAP, before it gets out of control.

Memories can evolve over time because of this, and you could say that this is why experience often leads to wisdom...our beliefs and models for how we look at the world evolve as we experience more life. Altering how we recall an event can help explain why therapy works for many people, as the therapist helps a person recall something, then helps them to interpret the memory in a different, more useful way.

Here is another example of fluid, hyperlinked memory: Many of us have an uncle we remember who told the same story at ever gathering, but every time he told it, he embellished it more and it became a wild and very tall tale. Your uncle did not mean to lie...he just kept linking up more and more details from his memory and people seemed to enjoy his stories...or maybe it was the case of Budweiser he drank...but you get the point. Memories are not perfectly stable recordings, they can mutate and link to other memories, and change based on what you are experiencing when you recall those old memories.

Could an environment, person, or familiar experience trigger a memory? Of course, and you have experienced this too. Most of have heard an old song that took us straight back to a time in the past, when we were perhaps driving with our friends one summer night and having an awesome time! To make the point, every time I hear "Dreams" by Van Halen, I remember cruising with my friend John in his dad's old Pontiac Catalina, singing along at full volume at a red light, in a turn-around on Fort Street the summer of 1986. The windows were down, people were looking at us, and we did not care. If you are lucky you have an experience like this, and maybe another song or two you remember listening to during a really great night with your love. It's not like this occurs just with music, any sense can trigger a memory. Many of us will remember being at a relative's house when we were younger if we smell a certain food cooking.

While those examples are pleasant, unpleasant memories can also be triggered too. Unfortunately, many of us also might hear something in the way our spouse says something and be reminded of a time when we were not treated well by someone...a parent, an ex-girlfriend, or whoever. We might immediately get triggered by that association and get pulled into the emotion from that experience, before we are even aware why our emotion is shifting.

On top of that basic trigger event, memories that have similar emotions to what you have recalled can be triggered too, because one memory might have an association to another, and another, and the emotions from those memories are triggered and we are off to the races! These things seem to take on a life of their own and just keep firing off as the memories rise up and further trigger chemical releases and the accompanying feelings and other similar thoughts. Even though this whole thing makes us seem like we might be crazy, this is very normal, and there are ways to manage it.

HOW TO BREAK THE NEGATIVE THOUGHT CYCLE

When this tsunami of memories and emotions starts to take over, we ourselves are the most qualified to pull ourselves out of it most of the time. Generally, we will be aware of our emotional state before anyone else, if we have learned to pay attention to ourselves (unless you are with someone who is incredibly sensitive). As soon as we feel the spiral beginning, we can interrupt the pattern in a number of ways. If you are not sure you have the necessary awareness, you could read about mindfulness meditation or talk to a therapist, and probably build your self-awareness. For some ideas about how to break the negative thought cycle, start with this:

- Notice and observe the thought.
  If you know what triggered it, try to laugh at how awesome your mind is to be able to make those associations and pull thoughts together that way! Then, think about something that feels good or that you are grateful for. Trying to not think about something just adds energy and self-loathing to the equation, because you will not be able to stop a thought that way and might beat yourself up for your lack of control. As an example: Do not think about a blue giraffe. It's impossible, so good luck with that!

- Do not attach more emotion to the thought or dwell

too much on it.

You do not have to go all the way and follow that feeling or memory just because the thought appeared. You can acknowledge that the thought and feeling happened, appreciate how awesome your brain and body is to be able to remember and respond that way, but then just let the feeling pass on its own. If you are chasing the unhelpful thought down a rabbit hole, deliberately think about something that feels good or that you are grateful for.

- Go for a walk outside or do something physical. Change the state of your body or where you are. Your mind will follow your body.
- Move some furniture around in the room you are in to change things up.
- Is there something you are looking forward to doing or going?

Try to imagine that thing in detail. A strong thought of something awesome can displace the old thoughts and make the emotions that accompany those thoughts weaker, through your change in focus. You do not shut down unhelpful thoughts by resisting them, you shut them down by thinking about helpful and wonderful things.

To summarize, do whatever you need to do to occupy your mind somewhat with something else that is not too important or related to any "problem" you are experiencing. Getting your thoughts on something that feels better than the old thoughts is your primary objective. It's your responsibility. And it's the best way for you to help yourself and those around you. Working your ass off on some project for a few hours or a weekend might help too. For one reason, engaging your mind on something else will interrupt the downward spiral, and for a second reason, finishing something feels pretty awesome.

You alone control what you focus your mind upon. The emotion you feel at any moment is direct feedback about the thing you are focusing on. Shift your focus until you find something that feels just a little bit better to think about so you can improve your experiences.

BELIEFS

Our beliefs are responsible for trouble, and victory. What we believe to be true, affects our perceptions, our motivation, and our actions. If we take common-sense approach, it is pretty easy to see that we will only give our best effort to do something, if we believe it is possible for us to accomplish that thing. If we think it not possible, we will not put forth our best effort, if we even try at all.

Below are some examples of how beliefs can affect us, either by limiting us, or by empowering us:

- A man sees a pretty lady, but believes she is "out of his league" and would not be interested in him.

Outcome: He spares himself the rejection by not talking to her at all.

- A boy thinks he is not good at sports.

Outcome: does not practice or try his best to get to the ball when playing.

- A man wants to start a business, but believes he needs a certain education to succeed.

Outcome: He stops before even starting his business.

- A girl believes she is a great actress.

Outcome: She memorizes her lines and practices for hours before the audition for the school play. She nails it.

What we believe can be compared to the classic question:

Which came first, the chicken or the egg? For fun, let us first start with the chicken! This is how people get beliefs:

We watch the people around us and absorb them, until we are about seven years old probably. There is a saying attributed to the Jesuits: "Give me the child for the first seven years and I will give you the man".

Later in life, adopting new beliefs goes more like this...

- Some event happens
- We make up a story to explain what happened and why.

Our mind wants to make sense of the event, so that it can help us figure out how to get more experiences like it, or to avoid experiences like it. The story we create is based on the things we remember about the event and things we perceived that led up to the event. All of these memories and perceptions are filtered through existing beliefs at that time, so they are not factual, or very reliable.

- Our minds will often over-apply the story we created as a way to frame the event in some familiar pattern. We try to draw conclusions and generalizations about an event based on the story we built around a previous unrelated or loosely related event. Sometimes it matches new experiences to old experiences in very strange ways. Your mind does this in the attempt to keep us safe.
- Yet another wrinkle: We tell ourselves this story anytime we are reminded of the earlier event.

Each time we recall the original memory, we attach a little bit more information to it based on our current situation, mood, thought or feeling related to that new experience that triggered the old memory. This expands the number of situations, memories, et cetera, which can trigger the memory.

Note: Even if we did not alter our memories every time we revisit them, the original memory was never complete or accurate because of our limited perspective at the time. Our existing beliefs act as filters to our senses every moment of every day. If you do not believe that your perception is filtered by your thoughts, look up some videos about *selective awareness test* published by Daniel Simons and Christopher Chabris, and really *do* the test, don't cheat!

- Finally: The belief you have colors how you perceive current situations, further supporting your existing belief.

Your mind *always* looks for evidence in the real world to support its beliefs. Your mind dislikes contradictions and loves consistency. It will do almost anything to avoid admitting errors in its belief or its model. It will filter out or ignore new information that contradicts its existing beliefs and models, until something causes it to open up to new possibilities. Often, it is a big life event such as losing a job, a break-up, a divorce, a death of someone close or other significant event that shakes a person up enough to have them question core beliefs.

During those times of change, there is uncertainty but there is also an opportunity to look at things fresh and to learn and grow as a person

It is during these times that a person can re-categorize or create different meanings for events of their lives and truly transform the way they approach life and relationships. In short, these events give us a second chance.

IT'S EASIER TO LOOK AT SOMEONE'S SPLINTER

(Instead of the Log in our Own Eye)

You can see how your beliefs about what is possible affect your own life, but it is often easier to see how their beliefs might affect the lives of others first. Many of us have a friend who says that they want to be wanted, to be first choice of their partner, and to be happy in that relationship. Yet, we see that friend repeatedly choosing to date emotionally unavailable men or women. People tend to fall in love with a person if they are somewhat attracted to them, spend a significant amount of time with them, and perhaps are not strongly involved with any other potential mates. When your friend continues to decide to spend time with this person, they are likely to fall for them or at least begin to believe that person they are spending time with is a significant part of their life and likely their future.

It might not be a conscious choice, but it is not happening by chance either. It could be that your friend does not feel worthy of real love, with the person they want to be with, so they put up obstacles, false ultimatums, and stories. It is as if that person does not believe in the possibility of being with someone, they enjoy who is available, and who also wants to be with them.

I am not saying that this is always the reason relationships do not pan out, as sometimes people are just following different paths, and they were only compatible with each other for a particular season of their lives...if this sounds like a situation you have been in, all I can suggest is to try to be grateful for the (hopefully) magical time that you likely enjoyed together, and that you aligned with each other and crossed paths at just the right time to allow you to have the experience and to grow from it.

QUESTIONS

Our questions determine much of our path in life. One simple way to challenge your existing beliefs is to ask better questions. When something happens that might be perceived as negative, ask yourself, different questions, like:

- "What is good about this situation?"
- "What do I really want now that I have this experience?"
- "How could this be better?"
- "What is possible?"

There is always some silver lining you can examine and pay attention to

HABITS

Our bodies provide transportation for our minds and spirit. The condition of the body, its chemistry, and state in any moment can have a major impact on how we feel, which in turn will affect our thoughts. Consider some common habits and how they affect how you feel and your thoughts:

- Watching TV for 10 hours a day will affect how you feel and what you think about.
- Reading books to learn about famous people who inspire you, or books that teach you something will also affect how you feel and what you think about.
- Being alone excessively or in contrast, developing friendships will also change the way you feel, think and act.

Your habitual actions will trigger thoughts and feelings that are associated with those actions. Your habitual thoughts will encourage similar feelings and thoughts too. If you are doing the same things, thinking the same things, and feeling the same emotions every day, you are not going to change your life. If you have the same inputs, you will get the same outputs.

Start with this

If you are not happy with areas of your life, making any change at all might be what you need to break a pattern and start feeling better. If you always sit alone at home after work, make it a point to do something different for a few weeks instead. If you sit in bed and watch TV, sit somewhere else and read a book or putter with a hobby you have not enjoyed for a while. Go to the

MICHAEL BLIZMAN

library and find a book to read. Go read that book at a coffee shop. Join a book club and talk about the books with new people. Join a gym. Go for a walk outside in your neighborhood or a bike ride. Write an article and post it on social media about something you find interesting or funny. Go to a different grocery store than your normal one. Do anything but do something different than you normally do to get out of your routine.

EXPECTATIONS

Our expectations contribute to everything we experience or unconsciously filter out. We basically experience what we expect, believe in, and focus on. Your mind wants to be right and will look for evidence to support existing beliefs and expectations. If you expect relationships to cause pain and not last, and you break up with your significant other, your mind gets to be right again: "See, I knew it wouldn't last." Somehow along the way, you probably did not pay attention to the enjoyment you likely experienced but focused on the thought it was too good to be true. You might have broken up anyway, but without the negative expectation, that event has a different meaning. Without the negative expectation, your mind might say instead: "I enjoyed many parts of that relationship and learned more about what I want and don't want in my next relationship." In either case, you might want to take some time alone and eat ice cream, but the length of time before you feel good is less without the negative belief. One more thing about this, if you lose the negative expectation, the next person you are attracted to will be less likely to have negative beliefs too, which will lead to more fun and more growth instead of a repeat of your previous relationship that started with a negative expectation.

Expectations often form the root of critical and annoying behavior too. When you expect someone to drop everything and focus on your needs to make you feel good, eventually you are going to be disappointed. People have their own agendas, preferences and lives to lead, and generally do not want to be influenced to ignore their own goals for someone else's all the time. When you are disappointed, you will probably lash out or become demanding or needy, trying to get the other person to behave the way you want them to. This repels people. If you want to be attractive, focus on things that make you happiest, and do not rely on others to fill you. If you are happier more of the time, other happy people will tend to show up in your life. It is a lot easier and more fun to be around people who do not need your attention to be happy and being together can add joy to lives of both because spending time together is drama-free and flows better.

YOUR STANDARDS

Raising your standards is a decision that makes you feel powerful.

Come up with a list of your own. Make a manifesto if you like! Here are some of mine that I have found useful at various points in my life.

- My work and level of service will be of the highest quality and delivered as quickly as possible.
- I invest my attention in people or situations which support me and my vision for my life.
- I build relationships with more experienced people who have similar goals or goals that complement my own goals, so that I can be pulled up by my association with those people and have an example to which I can aspire.
- I build relationships with people at my own level in various aspects of life so that I can feel camaraderie and acceptance.
- I build relationships with people who are not at my level in certain areas so that I can be a mentor or encourager to them.
- I honor the traits and core values that make me unique as well as my non-negotiable desires and vision for my life.
- In the past, I have sacrificed my values to keep the peace, comfort level, or status quo with others. From now on, accept me, walk with me, help me,

grow with me, or stay out of the way please.

- I align my daily goals with my core values so that I am pulled into action each day rather than trying to motivate myself constantly.

FOCUS: WHATEVER WE FOCUS ON, WE GET MORE OF

As my negative story continued, it is as if I was training myself to look for more evidence to support the story. And I found it! Then I found evidence to support other negative things in my life everywhere I turned. After a while, it begins to feel hopeless to change anything, because all you see is negative stuff to prove how bad people and the world are. When going through some difficult time, it is really important to try to pay attention to the things in your life that work or are going well and leave the negative things alone as much as possible to break the pattern a bit.

Start with this

If you are not sure whether or not you are having recurring negative thoughts about a person or situation, you can train yourself to be more aware. This might sound strange, but here is what I did: For a couple weeks, I carried a plastic spoon in the front pocket of my pants. Every time I thought something negative about a specific person, I moved the spoon to the other front pocket. By doing this, I became very aware of how often I was thinking negative thoughts. Once you determine how big a problem you have with negative thoughts about your partner, there are a number of ways you could break that old pattern or habit, some which are listed below, in no particular order:

- Think about anything or everything good you have in your life and feel grateful for those things.

- Leave the relationship. If you do not interact with each other anymore, you will not be triggering your old ways, and the negative thoughts will subside over time.

- Stop the negative recurring thoughts about your partner (the story you are telling yourself about the situation). Several times a day, or whenever a negative thought about your partner arises, tell your own mind, "thanks for sharing that", and immediately list several positive things you believe about your partner and remember that he or she is doing the best they can right now. Make a list of good qualities he or she has and have it ready for when you need it!

- Change the pattern of interaction so that you build positive associations of being with your partner.

- Do something new together or that you have not done for a long time. Find a way to laugh together as often as possible.

- When you are tired or hungry, or otherwise not at your best, pay special attention to your words. Pause a bit longer than normal before responding in conversation. It is OK to respond slower than normal. Remember...you are tired!

ACKNOWLEDGING OUR EMOTIONS AND ACCEPTING OURSELVES

You, me, and everyone else make the best decisions they know how to make at a given point and do what we know how to do at our current state of awareness and personal growth. Often, we do things to make ourselves feel safe from whatever we are not ready to fully accept or deal with. Everyone is doing the best they know how to do and judging them harshly is not helpful.

Often, our behaviors are a way to distract us from the feeling that we are afraid to feel. I spent a lot of time learning to think differently, and finally had to recognize that I was not going to be able to grow much more until I faced a couple things I had been unwilling to experience fully and accept. When you are ready, you might consider feeling it all completely. I see this as 2-part activity:

Part 1-After many years, I was finally ready to be with all the emotions I had been running from, numbing myself to. There were a couple things in my life that were so deeply painful that I avoided them. One night, actually about 3 in the morning, while I was sleeping alone, I finally sat with those events, the emotions they caused, and I experienced them fully. I did not try to justify those feelings or convince myself they were not valid. I did not attach to them or tell myself that I am those thoughts and feelings. I just felt them. While I did not look at the clock, I believe the emotional pain passed on its own actually in a few minutes. Granted I was sobbing for several minutes over a couple things I was trying not to deal with for so long, but they passed. After sitting with them fully and then observing the feelings pass, I marveled at how much better it seemed to just to experience them instead of hiding from them for so very long.

Part 2-I had to accept and actually LOVE all of those parts of myself that I recognized during Part 1. I had to accept and love even the really ugly parts of my character that I discovered along the way over all those years as I hid from my feelings. All the thoughts and actions I am capable of in order to avoid pain. I have to have compassion for myself. Out of that compassion for myself, I realize that we are all connected and experiencing similar things even if the individual experiences are different. I have no place to judge anyone else.

I am not perfect or done yet, but as I revisit and edit this book, I am reminded of the things that help me grow. If sharing this provides this value to even one other person, it was worth the hours spent writing.

WHAT WORKS

I find pure theory for its own sake to be dull. Sometimes I am interested in finding out why something works, after I prove that it works. Mostly though, I just want to apply the knowledge to make the most positive impact possible. My focus after each epiphany was to find a way to implement a positive change in one area as quickly as possible. If it works, I will use it, and maybe figure out why it works later. I want concrete actions that give predictable and repeatable results toward making my life better.

Below are the things I started doing. If something did not help me within a short time, I dropped it and replaced it with something different to try, or something that seemed to give a good result. Here is a brief list of the things I started doing which seemed to help me, and these things started helping me fairly quickly, and gave me momentum in a new and better direction:

- Journaling
- Meditating
- Reprogramming
- Resting
- Eating
- Moving
- Surrounding
- Reading
- Smiling

By sharing some details of what I experienced with each of these new activities, maybe it will help convince you to try them.

PRACTICE: JOURNALING

The gratitude journal is how I started. I listed 5-10 things to be grateful for every single day and wrote them in a notebook. I committed to myself to do this for 30 days. If it was going to work, it certainly would show evidence within 30 days, and if it did not, I could drop it forever. After Day 4, I grew weary of writing down the same boring things from previous days. You see, I am a complete smart-ass. So, I started out journaling by jotting down things like "delicious coffee" or "I woke up and walked under my own power", or "my F-cked up old car started without jumper cables". While all these things are wonderful, they can start to get repetitive and have an underlying tone of negative expectations.

After a few days, I wanted a break from repeating those same items each day. I think this is why the gratitude journal works so well! The boredom of those pat answers, coupled with my commitment to complete the 30 days of journaling, encouraged or forced my mind to look for new things to write in the journal the following morning. I think that is the secret of why the gratitude journal helps...your brain seeks novelty and if you are committed to make a journal entry tomorrow, you are training your mind to look for anything around you to be grateful for so you can write something new in the journal. The list grows, and you can see with fresh eyes all the great things you already have in your life. Once you are looking with fresh eyes, you start to see opportunities and possibilities that which are all around you. You get less blocked up with negative thoughts.

The next type of journaling I tried, I call, *"Column A, Column B"*

About 2-3 times a month, I would draw a 'T' chart on a page of the journal, and label the first column, "Inspired to..." and in the second column, "Awaiting further direction". A sample of this T-chart is shown below. I like to add this to my journal notebook and include the date I created it on the page.

Inspired to	Awaiting further direction
De-clutter my office	How to connect more fully with my teenage daughter
Call Bill to discuss the project he mentioned at the party	Manage my finances after my divorce without additional strain on my children
Join Toastmasters group	Get along better with Tim at work

In the first column, I would make a brief note about anything that had my attention, and for which I had a clear next step or action to take. For example, if I was annoyed by my closet being crowded and knew there were old clothes in there I would never use, I might enter something like, "donate extra clothes to charity". Or if I had an argument with someone and did not like the way I handled it, I might enter, "apologize to Emily for raising my voice". I think by writing these items in the first column, we are making our ideas tangible on paper, and setting an intention or goal deliberately, which makes it more likely that we will follow through. Further, it gives us confidence in our instincts and judgement about our own feelings. Our writing down these things clarifies them and makes our thinking and beliefs more aligned, and this makes our behaviors more consistent with following through on those things.

The second column is a bit different. In the second column, I write down things that might be on my mind, or bothering me, but for which I had no clear idea about how to proceed. If I had little money on hand, but the house needed maintenance, I might enter something like, "Find an enjoyable way to make repairs to the siding". If I was not getting along well with someone I had to travel with, I might enter something like, "Achieve a peaceful resolution with Bob", or "Find something to enjoy about traveling with Bob". I think this journaling helps because it lets you acknowledge a negative feeling about a situation honestly and gets it in front of you on paper.

Why I think it works: Seeing the problem described briefly on paper clarifies that the problem as something that is separate from you, and you can see it and understand it clearly. The scope of that problem is clearly written so it does not seem bigger than life anymore. Releasing the problem to this column in your journal, and stating that you are awaiting further instruction, gives your mind permission to chill out for a bit. By relaxing and releasing a bit, you are open to seeing solutions and look for new information which might provide some insight or idea toward a solution. I think just the act of writing it out gets the issue out of your head, so it does not block you up anymore.

Why it works barely matters...do it!

OK, all that previous explanation was for the fact-based, reasoning people out there who need to understand why something works. Sometimes things just work. Write out the things like I am suggesting and see what happens. Some of my experiences with this A/B journaling seem a bit outside of reason or coincidence. In other words, the concern that I released to Column 'B' got resolved in very unlikely ways, and ways specific to my need and experience and interpretation, but utterly satisfying and reassuring to me. By writing it down in Column B, you are essentially allowing some higher power to take ownership of that thing, so you can pay attention to and take action on things that you *do* know how to handle right now and just let go of the big problems for a bit. Often, it seems that a higher power just takes care of stuff for you without your direct effort or action.

I would describe or compare Column A/Column B journaling as much as a part of spiritual life as I would describe it as "psychologically useful"

When you do this Column A and Column B journaling, with full sincerity, you might be surprised by the way your problems get solved without you taking direct action. My experience with Column B miracles and synchronicities truly got my attention and opened me up further to possibilities I never imagined before. There are a lot of examples, but one week I was consumed by work and being a bit too serious. I wrote in my Column B journal that I wanted to have fun and laugh a bit with others. The next night I was working on this book while drinking beer at a taco place, and a nice lady asked me if I was writing a novel. We had a brief exchange and then she went back to hang with her sisters. They were having a good time and laughing, and I enjoyed the evening more just because of briefly meeting them. Another time, I wrote in column B concerns I had about an expense I believed would be hitting my bottom-line soon. Unexpectedly, about 3 weeks later, I received an out-of-cycle and significant raise at work that covered the expense. There are other examples, too. I used to be very closed off and very logical but let me just say that writing down my Column 'B' items in a dated page has proven to me that we are in a friendly universe and that something a whole lot smarter than me is able to easily coordinate things to help us if we are open to it. I get to look back in time and see things that were bothering me, and then recall how things worked out somehow along the way. I received all the benefits of this higher power help, and it had nothing to do with my actions, any religious habit, or even me acting in a morally immaculate way either...I still drink beer, yell profanity at my dog sometimes, and do stuff that is not "nice". I still have blessings overflow in my life. It is a demonstration of unconditional love from whatever higher power you believe in, and it makes me want to do and be better. Give Column A/Column B Journaling a try and see what happens.

PRACTICE: MEDITATING

If meditation sounds intimidating, think of it as sitting quietly in a chair instead. That sounds a little easier. At first while meditating, I tried to not think about anything. When meditating, I start by focusing on something really uninteresting like my breath, or an air conditioner droning on, or running water perhaps. When I started meditating, I became aware that it worked for about 10 seconds before some other thought would interrupt and demand my immediate attention. I became a bit frustrated and felt like I needed to try harder. Trying harder to meditate does not work out very well...it's like trying to crush the ball when golfing...you miss a lot. It's OK though, this is part of the process of learning.

Then I changed my approach. I accepted that disruptive or noisy thoughts are normal. Meditation helps because practicing it allows you to become aware of those thoughts. When a thought pops in, do not resist or fight it. Instead, notice that it is there and be grateful for your wonderful mind that is trying to help you in the only way it knows. Do not judge the thought as good or bad. Just gently shift your focus back to your breath, or the air conditioner or whatever you were paying attention to start your meditation. Here are two skills that improve through a mediation practice:

- With practice, your ability to deliberately change what you focus your attention on improves.

- With practice, your ability to notice thoughts and observe them improves. Consider this very logical statement:

The observer is separate from the thing that is observed

When you are observing a thought, it gives you the space you need to decide whether or not you want to attach to that thought or believe it.

My results from meditating

What happened after meditating for a while? After several weeks of consistently meditating for between 7 and 20 minutes every morning, I found myself less likely to react immediately to things that usually irritate or provoke me. It is like I finally noticed the space between a triggering event and my response, and I was able to be in that space. The space is always there, but when we are highly reactive emotionally, we ignore the space and just react with whatever is natural in that moment, even if that reaction does not match who we would like to be.

I noticed that after several weeks of meditation practice in the morning, that discussions or situations which previously would have led to anger or raised voices, often led to nothing but the end of a short exchange without escalation. I was much less reactive. The morning practice of meditation itself is quite enjoyable now too. It is nice to wake up and give yourself a few minutes to just be and enjoy some quiet time. Near the end of the meditation, I often am drawn or pulled into my morning routine, but in a relaxed, not a frenzied way. In addition to the morning session, I find that even a minute in the mid-day helps me perform my work better now as it helps me to focus my mind on one thing that I can take action on rather than the stress of all the problems at once.

Meditation (a.k.a. sitting quietly for a few minutes) helps in a number of ways. First, some days I have more intruding thoughts than other days while meditating. That is OK and totally normal. It happens to everyone and does not mean you are *bad* at meditating. Noticing the noise level in my mind helps me to be aware of how things are going in my life...more noisy thoughts just means I have more situations popping up that want some attention from me. Meditation helps by allowing space for new ideas and observations to surface without committing any of those ideas into my beliefs about how the world is, or how a person is, or any of that, unless I decide that thought is helpful to me. You get to experience every thought and feeling, without being controlled by them.

Start with this

Take 5-20 minutes every morning to do a guided meditation to slow down your thoughts. After a few weeks of doing this consistently, I began to notice my thoughts before they could take over and control the direction of my day. Before, when someone said certain things in a certain way, it was like a trigger and I would lose my composure or react like I was on autopilot...they pushed my button. At one point after a few weeks of meditation, that button was not so reliable anymore. The same type of trigger conversation or event, but I did not react like I did before. I was able to notice what was happening and respond in a way I chose. It was very satisfying.

If it seems strange to you to try to sit quietly and meditate, you can find some good guided meditations on YouTube for free. Most work best if you have headphones on as you listen, and if you can get yourself to a quiet place where you can relax. By using these in the beginning, sometimes it feels a little easier to go with the flow a bit and not feel weird. I prefer to meditate first thing in the morning before my mind gets pulled into other people's agendas and such, but anytime is a good time. I have done them on a morning break in my car, I have done them on a lunch break, and I have done them after work to reset before arriving home to my family. The simple act of sitting still and quiet gives your mind some time to process and organize things without any effort from you. As you focus on something not too interesting, like your breath, or an air conditioner humming, or peaceful instrumental music, you can begin to notice your thoughts arrive without getting emotionally involved in those thoughts. You can slow your thoughts down a bit to give time for you to consider if this thought feels good or not, if it helps you or not. And when the thought passes by, you let it go.

The thought is not you.

I think a meditation practice helps you to get a new habit of not getting attached to the thought. Often, we seem to think the thought we are having is *us*. When you observe a thought during meditation, you know the thought is not you, but is an experience you are having. You can notice the thought without judging if the thought is "true" or not. In the heat of a busy day, one thought leads to another and we scarcely pay attention to how those thoughts are developing, or if a bad feeling is gaining momentum or a foothold in us. One thought leads to another related thought and so on and so on. If they are helpful thoughts, it can be great, as you seem to find more reasons to be in a good mood throughout your day, which leads to momentum and flow. If they are thoughts that make us feel bad, and they gain momentum, all that happens is you feel worse and get a bad mood, which is kind of an inversion of being in a flow state. Somehow when in this unhelpful state of mind, more things happen to reinforce that bad mood you are having...it's like your life wants to prove to you that you have reasons for the way you are feeling. You get more experiences similar to the feelings you have from whatever you are focusing your attention on...if you are thinking about the jerk who bumped into your car, you will probably find more experiences that feel like that. If you are thinking about the friendly store clerk who helped you and smiled a lot, you will probably find more experiences like that.

I think that meditation teaches us how to interrupt unintentional, habitual negative thought patterns. Before you answer back that you suck at meditating, remember that all you really need to do is sit in a comfortable chair or lie down for 5-15 minutes and listen to your breath or a refrigerator running. When your mind wanders, you notice the thought and appreciate that your mind is really good at connecting things and pulling things up to try to help you. Then gently put your attention back to your breath or the boring noise you were listening to.

I recommend a daily meditation practice, and it helps a lot in the long term, but is not a silver bullet to help immediately with strong and disruptive thought patterns. For example, if you have recently experienced a significant, highly charged life event like a break-up, a job change, or family member who is ill, you should start meditating, but you might benefit from some other ways to disrupt your noisy, negative thought patterns. You might need a backup plan to help you settle down, so you can incorporate meditation into your daily routine.

PRACTICE: RE-PROGRAM

Self-talk

Notice what you say when you talk to yourself. How many times do you think or say out loud, "I am such an idiot"? Recognizing that you could have done something better or handled a situation better is a really good thing and is a first step to improving the way you handle things next time, but such negative expression and labeling yourself an idiot instead of focusing on a behavior is not helpful. Worse yet, calling yourself an idiot actually is removing your own accountability for your unhelpful actions…Of course you screwed that up and you will always screw it up, because you called yourself an idiot. If you shift from "I am such an idiot" to "I could have handled that better", you are leaving an opening to improve how you will handle things next time the situation arises and are making yourself accountable. If you really want to improve, you might incorporate these experiences into a journaling practice in the evening. As you spend a few minutes recalling what worked well that day and what did not work so well, you might write down something like this: I overreacted to … and got nervous about how to express myself. Next time I will take a breath and try to speak more clearly and honestly about that."

By identifying more desirable behavior, you are asking yourself to rise to a higher standard, and because you are writing it out, it will affect what you believe about your own abilities

Routines

As we do the same habitual activities each day, we experience many of the same things and see the same people. This same-ness triggers same thoughts and feelings today that you had yesterday and the day before, and you can get stuck in a rut. Some studies say that we have 60,000 thoughts a day, and 95% of those are the same thoughts you had yesterday and the day before. Most of us get up at the same time in the same room, brush our teeth with the same hand and drive to work on the same route, so it is normal to expect that these routines would encourage the same thoughts and patterns of thought. I am not saying that your normal day is bad or good but suggesting that if you change a few things that you do each day, you will change some of the thoughts and feelings you have. When you think differently, you will have a different experience that day than you otherwise would. This can have a huge impact on how happy we feel, even if we are not sure why that is.

Pay attention to how you feel while you are doing your normal routine activities. If you watch television in the morning, do you pay attention to it, or is television just background noise while you get ready for work? If you do pay attention to something on television, does that experience make you feel good, excited, fearful? As an experiment, try changing your routine by creating a playlist of favorite upbeat songs to listen to as you get dressed and brush your teeth. When you make this change, do it for at least a week and notice if your experiences or mood during the week change in any way.

If you normally stop by to chat with someone at work, pay attention to how that interaction feels. I am not saying to ignore people who are in a bad mood or are consistently negative, but perhaps limit your exposure to them and find other people or activities to enjoy more of your time during the day.

If you check Facebook to see how great everyone else's life is going daily (or hourly), notice how you feel while doing that. Do you feel tired? Jealous? Annoyed? Grateful that you can stay in touch so easily with dear friends? If you are not getting energized or helped by your FB habit, set a limit that you will not look at it except for 15 minutes after you are done with your workday and notice if you feel any difference during the day.

If you are normally working at a desk for most of the day, try to organize your day by the hour and set a task to get up and stretch at least once per hour. If possible, use a mid-morning and/or mid-afternoon break to take the long way around to the restroom so you can move your legs and calm your mind. Instead of standing in a long line for heavy cafeteria food every day for lunch, try to bring a lunch from home and use the extra time to take a short walk around the building or whatever is available. Or use the time to talk to people you work with but do not normally get to see.

Technology

I listened to subliminal positive affirmations all night with headphones. I saw no harm in this, and YouTube has many available for free. I did not remember my dreams for the past couple years. I did have some interesting dreams some nights and I think this subliminal stuff lead to some of those. After a couple weeks, I seem to remember waking up in a better mood than I had been before. I was doing more than one new practice at this time, so this is not a single-variable experiment. I believe the affirmations help.

PRACTICE: REST

Every night during periods when I have been feeling bad or struggling with negative emotions, I set aside eight hours for rest. As long as I was lying down ready for sleep, I could listen to uplifting audio books, podcasts or whatever I felt like doing...as long as I was horizontal and allowing sleep when it arrives. If sleep did not come quickly, that was great too, because I got to enjoy a podcast that made me laugh or smile, or maybe learn something. During certain tumultuous periods, I found myself waking up at 3 in the morning pretty often. I use technology to help me go with the flow when it happens. I always have an audio book, or a guided meditation, or anything soothing ready to play on my smartphone with headphones. By having this ready, when I do not sleep all the way through the night, I do not get frustrated or resist it anymore...instead I look forward to some pleasant me-time and stay relaxed through the night. Since adopting this habit, sleep often returns quicker than I expect. So quickly in fact that I set a timer to turn off my audio book at the 15-30-minute mark, so I can resume listening the next day without too much difficulty.

PRACTICE: EAT WELL

I ate lots of salad, a little fruit, good quality protein from eggs and chicken. When I wanted it, I would eat big fat burger or donut too. Nothing too extreme in any direction, just good choices most of the time, and less quantity, more quality. Sometimes I eat something sweet if I want it, but not habitually and not for the purpose of shifting my mood. I have read that eggs and pepper increase production of oxytocin, which can lift your mood. A nice omelet in the morning with pepper and some veggies is quite awesome and taking just a few minutes to prepare it sends a signal to your mind that you are worth the effort to create something for your own wellness and enjoyment. The indirect impact of this kind of behavior might be huge in retrospect...it is an example of self-care or self-love and when you take consistent actions that indicate self-worth, the belief that you are worthy might penetrate your subconscious. As you have heard before, faith without works is dead, and the corollary is also true. When you act a certain way, it reinforces your beliefs.

PRACTICE: MOVE

I went for one or two walks every day. 10 minutes leisurely walking is fine. I also did some light stretching every morning and evening. Moving your body will immediately change your mental and emotional state. Your mind will follow your body.

During a few months of an emotionally chaotic period, I developed severe sciatica symptoms from piriformis syndrome. It is likely that this was initiated by painting while standing on an extension ladder when I was not used to that work anymore, while wearing the wrong shoes for standing on a ladder (duh). That probably caused the muscle to go into spasm. I have done plenty of dumb things before, and I never had those kinds of persistent, awful symptoms, so I think that my emotions were making things way worse. I was under doctor's care for this and it was pretty bad because no position gave relief. Not much sleep going on for those months, but I allocated 8 hours of rest every night anyway. As the symptoms allowed, I started stretching 2-3 times per day. As I improved, I added other light exercise when I felt like it like bike riding, pushups and eventually went to the gym when I felt like it.

Almost anytime I am starting to feel stressed or down, going for a walk or jog, or to the gym makes me feel better almost immediately (5-10 minutes after warming up).

PRACTICE: SURROUNDING YOURSELF WITH GOOD PEOPLE

I surrounded myself with the happiest, funniest people I could find. If being around someone correlated with a smile by me or that person, I would be around them, period. If I felt more tired after interacting with someone, I kept my distance, period.

Tune into how you feel as you interact with people in your life. Pay attention to how you feel when you fake-interact by reading their social media updates. Does this interaction add to your energy, or pull you down? If you are doing something or spending time with someone who does not add to your life, consider changing the way you interact with them. If there are people you are acquainted with who seem to be exciting or interesting, find ways to reach out to those people and get to know them better. They may be part of your new circle of friends if you give this a chance. The main point is to increase the time you spend doing things with people you enjoy.

PRACTICE: READ

I read dozens of books about mindfulness, self-help, and positive stories about interesting or exceptional people. I read about people who do awesome things. These people should become my peer group or virtual mentors and be the ones I consider the new normal to whom I compare myself or better yet, aspire to. They should be the ones who I emulate. If you hear about or read enough about great outcomes and experiences people are having, your mind starts to believe that those experiences are normal. The inverse of this is also true, so consider not watching the headline news as they report a lot of violence and horrible things first thing in the morning.

On the better end of the spectrum, if the people you identify with from your reading and entertainment habits are having good lives, and yet you are not yet having good experiences consistently, your mind will notice the inconsistency. Your mind starts to register some cognitive dissonance with the difference between what you are paying attention to while reading and your own life. If you are making positive authors and great people your peer group or virtual mentors, it is as if your mind starts to guide you toward new experiences and thoughts that lead to more fun and personal growth. You may notice more opportunities to grow out of your old comfort zone, because you are seeing the examples of this in your reading and the people you are paying attention to. I cannot explain how it happens, but as your focus changes, new people and situations often enter your life in new ways, and you have a new opportunity through them to experience new things. Whatever you focus on and think about, expands.

PRACTICE: SMILE

I smiled at every single person I saw and looked for something specific to appreciate about them. I tried to do this for every person I noticed, all day, even if it was just a quick second. There is always something to appreciate in someone. Some people have very symmetrical features. Others have a contagious laugh or smile. Still others are totally focused in the moment talking with their toddler, and all of it is beautiful in its own way. Some people are clearly having a personally challenging day but are still receptive if you kindly hold the door for them. There is always something to appreciate about a person if you are looking for it.

Appreciation is completely positive and not tied to anything lacking in your life or negative things. Develop a habit of finding something to appreciate about everyone and terminate your thoughts about that person before adding the yeah-but that nullifies the thing you appreciate about them.

Outcomes of "the practices"

One huge difference I noticed in myself since experiencing the epiphanies and then taking up my practices described in the previous chapters is that while problems and challenges still come up, I am less likely react instantly based on whatever mood I might be in. In Victor Frankl's book, "Man's Search for Meaning," he makes a powerful statement:

> *"Between stimulus and response there is a space. In that space is our power to choose our response. In our response lies our growth and our freedom." —Victor Frankl*

Once the practices became habits, I noticed that there is usually a bit of space between the time I notice and experience a situation, and the time that I respond to it. For much of the past, certain situations would trigger an automatic response in me, and that response did not always serve me the best. Getting angry, afraid or sad automatically does not often lead to optimum behavior or help you relate to others. Sometimes now, instead of reacting, I ask questions of the other person involved, or sometimes I ask questions in my own mind that lead me to responding in a way that better supports how I want to present myself.

"Quality questions create a quality life. Successful people ask better questions, and as a result, they get better answers." – Tony Robbins

Asking better questions is a behavior you can start right now, without waiting for any epiphanies or any other habits to form.

It seems like a minor thing, but if we ask better questions when we talk to ourselves, it changes everything. Our minds look for answers to any question you pose and will provide answers to those questions. Sometimes there is an immediate feeling or emotional response when we talk to ourselves and ask questions. Have you ever tried to solve a problem and then got tired or frustrated enough to leave it alone for a bit and go do something else like go for a walk, shower, or even go to sleep? Sometimes the solution or answer just pops up later. Our mind keeps working in the background on whatever problem you were focused on and emotionally engaged with.

Your feelings tell your mind the topic is important, and your attention gives your mind direction. Your mind is like a genie that will respond to your self-talk, questions, and any task or problem you assign it. You assign the task to your mind by your focus and the intensity of your feelings. Our minds go looking for the solution to whatever you have asked without judging if the answer will be benign or harmful. You are in charge.

If you your thoughts include questions like, "Why do only bad things happen to me?", your mind will look for answers to that question, and will provide observations from the world around you to prove that you are only worthy of bad experiences. If you ask a question like, "What would it be like if everything was working out for me?", your mind will tend to look around for observations that answer that.

Rather than asking a sad and useless victim-based question like, "why did I have to go through this?" or "why did this happen to me?" or "why am I such an idiot?"; instead, commit to asking something better. Instead of those types of questions, try to ask questions of yourself that will give answers which might serve you better. To help you get started, try some of these questions the next time a challenge arrives:

- What is good about this?
- What might be good about this?
- How could things get better?
- What is being drawn from me in this situation?
- How must I grow or what must I become to get past this?

CONNECTING THE DOTS

For those who are struggling and thinking that nothing works to get them out of their funk, I will offer this: You got where you are slowly, and you might not find your way as quickly as you hope. You will see great things happen early as you make changes, and continually if you keep on your journey. Here are the baseline behaviors that I think kick-started some positive changes and I suggest you try these ideas:

- Get a notebook and write in it every single morning or evening.

Write at least 10 things you can feel grateful for. This trains your mind to look for things to put in that journal, so you look for good things all day. Also consider doing the "Column A, Column B" journaling described earlier.

- Read books about subjects and people you are interested in or think you might be interested in, or who have awesome stories.

They can be non-fiction, they can be self-help, but they don't have to be. These are your new virtual mentors.

- YouTube has lots of free motivational videos.

Find some that pump you up. Anthony Robbins, Les Brown, etc. Listen to them when you are not engaged in other activities like when driving, waiting for eggs to cook, or whenever. This will help keep your level more upbeat than your current default setting.

THINGS I HAVE LEARNED ALONG THE WAY:

At times, I have over-invested in relationships with people who did not earn that priority in my life. I learned that I can lose perspective, act like a person I do not want to be, and that I can lose my confidence in those situations. As a result, I have more compassion now for others who are going through similar seasons in their lives.

What we focus on expands and becomes more important or true for us. If we constantly imagine and envision negative outcomes, we will tend to notice the bad things around us, and actually will create those self-fulfilling prophecies. The same is true for positive expectations...they tend to self-fulfill.

When we mostly focus on, imagine, envision positive outcomes and expect those things, incredible synchronicities or miracles become more frequent. Recognizing them and being grateful for these things seems to encourage those positive things to happen more often.

When we do not feel worthy or deserving of something, we will often sabotage ourselves, often, when we are likely on the verge of getting the thing we want.

We tell ourselves stories about our lives and situations. We incorporate these stories into how we identify ourselves...who we believe we are. People also have a need to be consistent. If we have helped a person before, we are more likely to help them again. If we have been doing something for a long time, or in a relationship with someone for a long time, we might exaggerate our feelings or affection for that thing or person, to make ourselves feel more consistent or authentic...if you have been dating for 2 years, you *must* be in love, right? If you are not in love, you might judge yourself as not being quite so put-together or as high-standard as you would like to believe you are! The truth is, growth happens at its own rate for each person, and sometimes things just do not work out the way you hoped at a certain time. Maybe things don't work out because you have something in yourself that needs work and attention before that good thing can show up in your life. A better story when this happens, is to believe that you are being cared for and that situation that ended was not in your best interest, and that a better situation is on its way to you. If that situation or person is truly for you, you cannot lose it, so relax a bit and be open to what is happening in each moment.

Recurring thoughts appear to be true, and to be our own voice or person. But we can observe our thoughts and our feelings. If you can observe something like you can observe a dog running, or a car moving, that thing you are observing is not you. You can observe your thoughts, so your thoughts are not you. Go ahead and notice your thoughts and experience your feelings. But do not believe that those thoughts and feelings define you. They can change and they can pass, and when they pass, you will still be there.

It is possible to bottle up our emotions for a very long time. Ignoring these so that you can continue working on projects, keep up your routines, avoid confrontation, and avoid that thing you are afraid of may eventually cause you great suffering.

When you block out pain and fear, you also cut off joy and connection to others.

It is likely that you could go into a full flat spin in your life if you block your emotions for too long. Eventually your spirit will feel like it is gone from you, and you are just a shell. Your spirit could rise up and demand attention from you...when it screams loud enough, every aspect of your life is open for radical changes, and you may or may not want to deal with all of that. I caught my bottling just before I believe I would have imploded my professional life, and possibly become a truly absent father.

Fear and doubt cause massive pain in this world. I have experienced sign after sign that I am being protected from the worst things that can happen. In short, every time I have been open to it, I have noticed the right people or right situation happening in my life at just the right time for me. It seems like over and over, God or the Universe or whatever you believe in, was telling me to stop doubting and just believe that I was going to be led to just the right circumstance for me to grow to my next level.

I am no guru, as I have no idea what level I am at, or what level I am moving to. I just know that I am growing now. I know that fear and doubt were dominating my mind at certain points in my life, and this caused me to be disconnected from my intuition, and the opportunities that are always surrounding me. Because of fear and doubt, I clinged to people and situations that did not serve me anymore. If I had more faith that I was being led and protected, I would have had less resistance to the changes as they arrived and would have experienced and caused less pain along the way.

We all crave to feel like we are consistent and authentic, and true to ourselves. Once we start down a path, we tend to try to stay on that path, even if we see signs that path conflicts with some of our priorities or values. In order to stay consistent and avoid admitting that we are making a poor choice, or going the wrong way for us, *we will even shift our beliefs and values* over a long enough time to try to align ourselves with the actions we have been taking and the decisions we have been making. We will do almost anything to not be wrong, even if the path we are on leads to shipwreck!

Something that really helped me when I finally accepted it is this:

There is a spark of God or something divine in all of us. We love, create, give and forgive.

Loving, creating, giving, and forgiving are examples of how we are made in God's image. These represent our highest selves. Our feelings and emotions are a gift to help us navigate life. How we feel matters. It is our duty to do what we must do to achieve a baseline of gratitude, contentedness, and well-being. If we do that, then we will notice when we feel any negative emotion as it will contrast with our normal state. Negative emotions arrive because we are focused and thinking about something in a way that is different from the way the best version of us sees things (or the way that divine spark in us sees things). That emotion is there to get your attention, so you can find a better path to follow. Pay attention to how you feel and ask good questions to figure out your next step.

CLOSING THOUGHTS

If reading this book has provided at least one or two actionable ideas for how to improve the way you approach some part of your life, it was worth the effort to write, and for you to read.

Some other things that are most certainly worth the effort, are to learn how to be still, to accept yourself fully, to clarify the things you want to be, do, and have; and to be compassionate to everyone, as they are just like you. They are doing the best they can do in the current moment with their current level of awareness. We are all both student and teacher to one another.

The subtitle of this book is, "Start with this." This book represents a starting point of how I began to move in what feels like the right direction for my life but is not intended contain any final lesson on the subject, or a final destination.

You may reach me here:

http://midlife-awakening.com/
michael.blizman@midlife-awakening.com
(281) 594-7528

Made in the USA
Columbia, SC
04 November 2023